Mapping Your Career Success

A workbook to help you plan a fulfilling career

DETOUR →

Carol Evanoff

Published in the United States of America by
Fair Winds Publishing
P.O. Box 220 Port Gamble, WA 98364
www.carolevanoff.com
First edition, September, 2011
Printed in the U.S.A.

Cover and book designed by Oriana Green

By Carol Evanoff

This book is dedicated to Jean Black
and Mrs. Clarke (my second grade teacher)
who both believed in me.
I never forgot what Mrs. Clarke wrote
on my report card:
"Carol never gives up on a problem."

Table of Contents

CHAPTER ONE
Away we go!

You're on quite a trip

Whether or not you've thought of it like this, **your career path is certainly a sort of lifelong journey**, and stops along the way are your various jobs. You may have meandered around without obvious destinations, or perhaps you've fallen by the wayside and are stuck in a deep rut.

Then again, maybe you've been on a long straight road that you're just realizing is going nowhere—**or at least not anywhere you truly want to go.** This book has been designed to help you navigate the complex map of your work life and help you attain fulfilling positions that can lead you on a clear route to job advancement and satisfaction.

As the traveler on this journey, you don't need to take this trip alone.

✔ Think of me as your travel agent, ready to make suggestions and help you make your travel plans.

✔ Think of this book as your guidebook to understand the world of career analysis and planning.

✔ I'll also show you how to enlist other allies to help you achieve your career goals.

Does this topic surprise you? Did you realize that people like me can help you scrutinize your job history in order to improve the quality of the job you already have and prepare for even better ones? It's been a very rewarding career for me, and I'm thrilled to be able to share with you what I've learned over my 35 years of helping others.

Where I became an expert in blasting roadblocks

I need to say a few words about the huge corporation where I spent my entire career. Back in the early 1970s most corporations were male-centric operations; men were in charge. Looking back, I probably could not have picked a more male-centric operation to join than a defense contractor who supplied the U.S. military. This organization was driven by technical knowledge and a high level of secrecy. Back when I first started there, women primarily worked the assembly lines and some low-level secretarial jobs, but held precious few positions of authority. This was a man's world, run by white men who wanted to keep it that way. About that time the world started changing, and along came Carol Evanoff and others to upset those tidy corporate applecarts. Over the ensuing decades a lot of apples rolled, and that makes me extremely proud to know I had a significant impact on the livelihood and overall well-being of so many people by helping them overturn their own carts.

Throughout this workbook I'll share stories of people who overcame tremendous obstacles to create their dream careers. Of course, I've changed their names and disguised their identities—to protect their privacy and so I can write honestly about the conditions we had to deal with. **But the lessons learned are very true, and I believe they'll help you to succeed despite whatever boulders may have landed in your path.**

How I came to write this book

A couple of years ago, the company I worked for decided they could get better performance from employees if they spent time training leaders. About 300 leaders attended this off-site class on mentoring. The instructor asked people to talk about both good and bad mentors they had experienced. After these leaders started to share their stories, one of the attendees stood up and introduced me to the group. I had been this fellow's mentor for most of his career, and he explained how my mentoring had a positive effect on many people in our

company. Then he asked everyone there who had ever been mentored by me to stand. Over 100 of the managers stood up, which certainly shocked the instructor.

That day it really hit me, that despite my various job titles and responsibilities, what I had primarily spent the majority of my own career doing was career mentoring, teaching and coaching people from many different backgrounds.

My main focus was on women and minorities, because the playing field in our large company was far from level. In order for those employees to succeed they needed special coaching, and they needed to develop clear strategies for success.

That's what drove me to create this guidebook, to help you find your way to your own rewarding career—especially if your playing field isn't so level either. Because most white males have their "good old boy" network to create advantages for them, **my main focus is to help women and minorities and to teach them strategies to be more competitive.**

Bursting through barriers

First, I'd like you to meet Julie. When I initially saw her, she was a beginning salaried employee working for my boss as an administrative assistant. It soon became obvious to me that Julie was very talented and had excellent leadership skills. I asked her if I could work with her to shape her career, so she'd eventually end up in leadership. At first she was skeptical, but she was willing to talk about it.

We met over the next month and began going through the process you'll see explained in this book. We started to design a career path for Julie by identifying her weak areas and getting her the specific kinds of experience she needed to strengthen her as a candidate for better positions.

I call this **career gap analysis**, but don't let that mouthful scare you or deter you from learning more about it.

It really is the magic passport that can unlock and apply all your personal potential for success.

Next we worked with other leaders in our organization to give Julie assignments that would provide growth opportunities for her to become an outstanding leader. She filled in for one manager while he was on vacation, and then she volunteered to head up a team presentation on a difficult project. All along the way she remained on the lookout for ways to gain new skills and polish existing ones. Instead of retreating from a challenging new computer program, she did tutorials on her own time. As she became the go-to gal for everyone else on her team who needed to use the program, her own self-confidence grew. Julie discovered she liked the empowerment that came from excelling, and she quickly realized how she could now control and direct the course of her career—rather than feeling at the mercy of those in higher positions who may not even know she existed. Her growing competency did, indeed, bring her the kind of positive attention that helped her progress from level to level.

Within a year she was promoted to a supervisor position, and within five years to a managerial position. More recently Julie was promoted to a director in our company, overseeing hundreds of employees with a huge annual budget and numerous travel opportunities, which is something she especially enjoys. Julie is also an African-American who's had to overcome the many obstacles you find in large organizations that are typically white and typically male. Yet she's flourished in that environment—

because she had a plan and kept following it, year after year. **Now she's enjoying a career that far exceeds her early ideas about what she might accomplish.** And the benefits of her success flow back to everyone around her—on and off the job—who see Julie as a role model for what can be achieved when you look beyond roadblocks that you may find in your path.

Do you know where you are?

Before we go any further into the process, let's take a moment to see where you are right now. By the time you've made it all the way through this workbook, I think you'll find it fascinating to see where you were when you began. So let's put some pins in your map.

How happy are you with your current position? (Five being very happy, three being somewhat happy and one being not happy at all.) Circle the number that most closely matches how you feel:
1 2 3 4 5

How did you end up in this job? (Did you actively seek it, was it supposed to be temporary, did someone else pressure you into it, was it a compromise of sorts?) Describe the circumstances around getting the job you now have:

_____

_____

_____

Have you ever thought about trying to get a different job? (Have you let yourself give up on that idea because of the economy, fear of failure, because others tell you to stay put, or other reasons?) Identify what you now believe are your top three roadblocks preventing you from finding a better job:

_____

_____

_____

_____

_____

Perhaps you uncovered a surprise doing that exercise, or maybe you've reaffirmed you like where you work now. Either way, **you'll still want to create a career map for yourself that lays out possibilities for advancement.** No matter how much you may enjoy your current position, over time you're bound to grow bored and your skills may stagnate. Now some people are just driven to accelerate their career progress as

much as possible. They're highly ambitious—whether for pride of personal accomplishment, competitiveness or a need to provide for their families. While other people are content to move along at a more leisurely pace. Either approach can make good use of the process in this book. You can hop a jet to get to your next destination, or you can get there by putting one foot in front of the other. It's totally up to you. I have no desire to add pressure to your life— just the opposite. **I want to make your life better by showing you how to maximize your potential—but always at your own speed.**

Gaining a competitive advantage

Early in my career, my company created mentoring programs for select employees. Each year they would choose some employees for these mentoring programs to develop their leadership skills. From the beginning I volunteered for as many of those kinds of mentoring relationships as I could. In working with the people in these programs, I developed the processes in this guidebook. What I saw over the years was **that my mentees really did have an edge over people assigned to other mentors who worked in a different manner.** Sometimes all it took was getting an employee to take a single class which made the difference in the job selection process.

Becky is a great example of that. She was competing with five other people for a leadership position, and during the course of her rotation into my division, one of the

things we determined she needed was a class in Cost Account Management. We made arrangements for her to take the class at a community college, and when the next job selection was complete, **it was that one class Becky took that ended up getting her the promotion**.

This is the kind of strategic thought that needs to go into your career planning with your mentor and your manager. They need to work with you to try to make sure you get the kind of experience and education you need. (And don't worry, I'll show you exactly how to enlist their help.) This process of going through this workbook will teach you those skill sets and can even assist your manager and mentor.

From layoff list to leadership

The other way I found this workbook strategy to be successful was in helping people who were rated at the bottom of the organization and were already on a layoff list. I've always championed people who didn't seem to be competing on a level playing field, whether due to gender, race, age or other challenges in the very homogenous corporate environment I found myself in. That was the case with two African-American men were going to be laid off from their division. In the first case I asked if I could move one of these men into a leadership position that I had open in my division. Once Ken made that transfer, we started going through the workbook steps and did the analysis to try to strengthen his abilities and his experience. One especially weak point was his fear of speaking to even very small groups. Though a really bright guy, his shyness had kept him from defending or even presenting his ideas. During the first year we developed plans together, these are a few of the things we did:

　　★ He went to classes to improve his communication tools

　　★ I coached him on a daily basis to improve his leadership skills.

　　★ I also made sure he received assignments that would cause him to stretch his abilities, such as leading increasingly complex projects.

Once he overcame his fear of sharing his ideas, he was transformed into a dynamo of innovation. His former manager

couldn't believe this was the same Ken he'd been ready to layoff. And of course, he wasn't! Ken began to smile more, his laughter could be heard down the hall, he started to take more care in his professional appearance, and in short—**nearly every facet of his well-being was impacted by the changes he made**. By the second year I was getting requests from other divisions for Ken to compete for their open positions. In that short amount of time he went from a low-performing employee to a high-performing leader who was sought after for promotions. When the right opening appeared for Ken, I was happy and proud to send him on his way to an exotic new location, confident that he had packed in his luggage a whole new skill set that would serve him well for the rest of his working life.

　　The next situation involved a Human Resources professional who was also rated at the bottom of his department. Since I had a position where I thought I could develop him, I asked if Juan could transfer to my division. Once again we navigated the analysis and coaching process with action steps:

　　✔ He read numerous books which I gave him to address some of the weaknesses we identified during his daily coaching.

　　✔ He studied the many different systems for employee evaluation.

　　✔ He became adept at interviewing and began to hone his ability to spot his own diamonds in the rough.

　　✔ We identified the kinds of assignments he could volunteer for in order to grow his abilities, such as offering to train new employees in his department and developing better employee handouts.

Within five years Juan was promoted to a manager in Human Resources, and a few years later he was moved up to Director of Human Resources at one of our other companies on the East Coast. Juan is thriving in that position, and while it saddens me to wonder how many other talented people never get the chance to reach their full potential, I'm thrilled that I was able to help Juan reach his.

Righting some wrongs

The most important reason I wrote this book came out of my sense of what is fair. When I began working for the huge corporation where I spent my entire working life, I found the good old boy network to be very strong. It quickly became apparent that the white males in charge routinely promoted only other white males. In 1978 this company had 30,000 employees, of which 48% were female, yet **only a small percent of those women were in leadership positions**.

This gives you an idea of what I was up against as I began to contemplate how I could help women and minorities advance in the organization.

Seven years later I was promoted to manager, and I was only the 30th woman to become a manager at this large corporation. **At that time I promised myself I would do all I could to mentor women and minorities to help them grow and succeed.**

A nice problem to have

During my first year as a manger I had 120 men and women working for me who were all mechanics and other specialized workers. Because I had started in the shop environment as an hourly employee, I really had an interest in doing what I could to nurture these women in the same way that I had been developed. To start the process I examined job classifications in the entire organization as well as across our company, looking for positions where I felt these employees could stretch their abilities and be promoted. **That's when I started creating this gap analysis process.** First I learned what each position required at the entry-level. My main focus at this point was educational opportunities for my employees. There were numerous classes at the junior college level that were available for these

Sadly, only .02 % of women had been promoted to leaders.

women to take, which could qualify them for some of these other positions in the company. Some of those jobs were working in stockrooms, as inspectors, schedulers, planners and more. I even tutored some employees in algebra to help them meet their goals of getting an AA degree.

Within the first or second quarter of their schooling, these employees qualified for the next position we'd mapped out for them. What I didn't anticipate was the magnitude of the success of this process. The year after we started, I had to hire another 30 employees to replace all the people who were getting promoted! That was a happy challenge I was delighted to meet.

As my own career progressed and I assumed more and more responsibility, I continued to use this process. There were many times when almost the entire group of people I worked with left my division for new jobs as they grew and filled in the gaps in their careers. With that kind of success, I was being sought after by many women in the development programs to mentor them.

These were often women who'd been working for the company for a long time. They were frustrated because they wanted to be promoted to leadership positions, but it just never happened and they didn't understand why.

One of the things I discovered was they hadn't fully documented their work experience in a meaningful way. **What this created were *perceived* gaps in their experience by those in charge, who used those gaps to justify not promoting them.** In one case, Della had worked in lots of the different quality assurance programs, including supplier quality assurance. When I met with her manager to find out what else she needed to advance, they said she didn't have enough technical background. So I met with her and reviewed her experience and we charted everything she'd done in her career. After this analysis it became very clear to me—and to her boss—that **she already had the technical experience she needed to get promoted, but she hadn't documented it in her files**. After we corrected that, she was quickly promoted to a Senior Manager.

After she was promoted, Della began to use the same process that I used with her with the people she began to mentor. By

encouraging my mentees to become mentors themselves and pass on the benefits, I was able to affect an ever-growing pool of employees. Over time, we all witnessed more and more women and minorities succeed in our workplace.

I won't lie to you—this will take some effort!

When you first consider this process it may seem daunting, but I urge you to stay with me and allow me to guide you through it step by easy step. **If you are diligent and follow the path laid out in this guidebook, I'm certain you can effect wonderful changes in your career, and by extension, in your life.** Advancing in your work life, becoming proud of your accomplishments and growing in self-esteem is a great boost to all areas of your life. Plus, it allows you to be a positive role model for those you work with, your friends and even your family.

What I've found is **those who are willing to put in the effort to go through this process will succeed**. One woman who read through the process with me and felt that it was too much work to do, decided instead to just keep looking for a better job. Five years later she ended up back in my office after wasting all that time merely transferring from one job to the next, never building her career the way she could have if she'd gone through the process. Finally, she was able to see that, and better late than never, she did embark on her own journey to a more satisfying career.

So how about it? **Are you ready to set off on an adventure that will change your life for the better?** Come on—it'll be fun as well as enlightening. Grab your passport and let's get going.

CHAPTER TWO
Planning Your Trip

Deciding what to take with you

When you prepare for any trip you pack your bags, but **for this trip, what you *don't* pack is just as important**. Especially if you've been working for a few years or more without seeing the kind of advancement you'd like, you've probably accumulated some negative ideas about yourself and your abilities. Here's how that might look:

• **You've been vaguely told you lack the necessary skills to succeed.** (Yet no one told you what those skills are or where and how to get them. This process will help you identify all that.)

• **Or perhaps your supervisor was specific and said you lacked leadership potential.** (You should know that those sort of statements are often very subjective, quite personal and may not be based on real assessments. In this book you'll learn exactly how to prove your potential.)

• **Maybe you just don't know where to look within your organization to find opportunities for advancement.** (Sadly, lots of companies still reserve those for the employees who've been deemed special enough for nurturing toward promotion.

Now you have an advantage—a guidebook to show you the way.)

• **Some people develop low self-esteem after years of being told they aren't performing tasks correctly or to a high enough quality level.** (And those people are rarely offered training or mentoring to overcome whatever it is they lack in order to succeed. After this process, those mysteries will be solved.)

• **You may have watched as less-talented co-workers or employees with less seniority were promoted past you.** (Though you probably don't know what

happened behind the scenes to cause that, from now on you'll have more control over that.)

• **Perhaps you've convinced yourself you're not smart enough to figure out the complexities of corporate politics and wade through them to get ahead in your career.** (While it may seem easier to stop trying and fade into the background, a better long-term solution is to beat them at their own game. I'll show you how.)

So do any of those situations resonate with you? If not, I bet there are other ways in which you've been made to feel inadequate or perhaps inferior to your co-workers. To insure old ideas don't weigh you down, let's get them out in the open. **Make a list of the ways you've been made to feel bad about your career, your abilities or yourself as a person.** These

may be things said to you by a boss or co-workers or something you surmised from the way you've been

treated. It could even be a self-image that started back in school or originated in your family. Unfortunately, not everyone gets a set of cheerleading, you-can-be-anything sort of parents. Writing this list may feel good—just putting it on paper can make it less burdensome. Or it might make you angry once you see all the negativity collected in one place. Don't worry, we're not going to dwell on this—think of it as spring cleaning—you'll feel much better when it's done.

make sense of everything. Then I realized I needed to give those feelings away or they would affect my performance. So after writing down the list or feelings I would crumple up the piece of paper and throw it in the trash can. Inside my mind I let go of the negative feelings and then I could move on.

Leaving that baggage behind can drastically shift you into optimism and hope and help you see the glass as half full instead of half empty. Try experiencing the word "no" as meaning "not now." That makes a big difference, doesn't it? **Many successful people will tell you they never hear the word "no."** It is doubtless said to

Phew! **Here's the good news: all of that is baggage you do NOT need to bring with you on our adventure to a better career.** Think of it as old information that no longer applies to you (and may not even have been true in the first place). From this day forward, all you're going to pack for your trip are:

✔ positive visions of your future

✔ your authentic skills that we'll document

✔ new tools you'll acquire in this guidebook

Getting rid of my own baggage

As you might imagine, when I was a very young woman working in a male-dominated environment I didn't get much if any encouragement from my bosses, co-workers or subordinates. I can recall numerous times when I would write down how I felt on a piece of paper, trying to

them, but people with a positive mindset react to it differently. They hear "maybe" or "ask me later" or "not me but someone else will." **They simply don't allow a two-letter word to stop them in their tracks.**

When comedian Rosie O'Donnell is asked by young people if they should go into show business, she always says a loud "no." Because she knows in order to succeed in that cutthroat industry you have to be tough as nails and can't let a few hundred people saying "no" affect you. She believes you have to want that kind of career so badly that nothing will stop you. If hearing her say "no" causes them to give up, she knows she did them a favor, because they never would have survived the emotional brutality of show business.

Luckily, most businesses are more benign. Still, when asked one time what I didn't understand about the word "no", I replied: "the stupid part." **I urge you to let all the old negativity go and move on; only pack the positive baggage to take on your trip.**

Think about what value you add to your company

That may be a new idea for you—especially if you haven't been treated as if you have special value to contribute. Yet you're a combination of attributes that make you one-of-a-kind with a unique contribution to make to the world. Sure, there are assembly line type jobs where it may seem like workers are interchangeable and disposable—and perhaps unenlightened

management sees it that way. **But the truth is, in every work situation many factors influence your success.**

Let's look at a few of the ones you may not be thinking about.

Temperament:

These are traits that define you and may be difficult to change (though to some extent, they can be improved). These are aspects of yourself that probably seem like they've just always been a part of you. Even though these are polar opposites, **circle whichever trait in each pair feels closest to your truth.**

- easygoing or irritable
- optimist or pessimist
- timely or tardy
- orderly or chaotic
- sunny or grumpy
- diligent or goof-off
- generous or stingy
- caring or distant
- joiner or loner
- persistent or sporadic
- sensitive or tactless
- open-minded or narrow-minded
- eager or hesitant
- dependable or flaky
- trustworthy or devious
- kind or undermining
- other key qualities you have:

_____

_____

_____

_____

_____

_____

_____

_____

What kind of picture does that paint of you as a person? As someone to work alongside? Are there any traits you'd like to modify? **Note them here:**

_____

_____

_____

_____

_____

_____

_____

_____

_____

_____

_____

_____

_____

_____

Personality:

Your temperament is who you are when you're all alone in a room; it's who you are at your core. **Your personality is how you express those traits with others.** How would your co-workers describe you? Don't know? Ask some! I bet there'll be some surprises. Are you perceived as someone who pitches in to lighten the load, or are you a clock watcher who leaves at five sharp no matter what? Do you genuinely care about your co-workers' lives, or are you sick of hearing about everyone else's star grandchildren? Do you make people smile and laugh, or do they tend to avoid you when they see you coming? Do you ask your boss how you can help with an important project, or do you hide in the breakroom and hope she doesn't give you a new task to do?

Write a few lines that honestly describe your personality on the job:

Innate talents:

We all have them, even if you've never written them down. Maybe you love doing **detail work** of all kinds—you love to immerse yourself in a big project with many moving parts because simple tasks bore you. That's a specific talent that has high value in the workplace, and you either have it or you don't. Taking a job that requires a lot of that when it's something you hate is not the road you want to be on. Or perhaps you're a great **organizer**, able to see the full scope of any project or situation. Logistics is your middle name. Again, another highly valued talent that you may not have told anyone you possess. Maybe you're an idea person, the most **creative** being in any group—you're the one who can design everything from inventory systems to get well cards. Or are you the one who loves to **solve problems**— you've never met a situation you couldn't make better. In this day and age, possessing inherent aptitude for **technology** is a highly prized talent—if you love to tinker with computers or other hardware, have you fully developed that talent?

These innate talents can give you a good idea about the kind of work you'll

find fulfilling. So take some time to write down your own innate talents:

_____

_____

_____

_____

_____

_____

_____

_____

_____

_____

_____

_____

_____

_____

_____

Social skills:

Are you the one who keeps track of all the birthdays in the office and remembers to bring in a card for all to sign? Do you encourage your boss to have a company picnic or retreat? Do you help plan it? Are you the one who always knows the right thing to say when someone has a personal crisis? Do your co-workers confide in you? How would you rate your social skills from 1-10? _____

Communication skills:

Are you good at getting your needs met because you aren't afraid to clearly state them? Do most people generally understand what it is you want when you ask them to do something? Or do you find yourself always explaining everything over and over? Does your supervisor ask you to help draft important reports or documents? Are you chosen to speak for the group when they have concerns that need addressing? Do you enjoy expressing yourself in writing? Do you volunteer to give presentations? How would you rate your communication skills from 1-10? _____

All of these things are part of the value you bring to every job you have—as long as you *use* your talents and skills. Looking at everything you wrote in this section, try and summarize in a paragraph what value you bring to work with you every day. This **Value Statement** is something we'll return to again and again.

_____

_____

_____

_____

_____

_____

_____

_____

_____

_____

_____

First let's take a fantasy trip to anywhere

In a perfect world, where there are no limiting factors like age, experience, education or opportunity, what would your ideal job look like? Do you work at a huge

multi-national corporation with the prospect of international travel? Or would you prefer a smaller, more intimate family-owned company where you know everyone's name? Do you work closely with a team of people who are your peers, or are you an executive sequestered in your own office? Do you prefer the slower pace and lower pressure of an intermediate level job? Or do you think you'd thrive in a fast-paced, high intensity, demanding position? Do you like to tell other people what to do, or are you happier when given directions? Would you

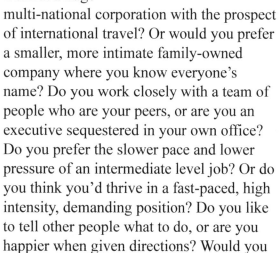

like people to look up to you and admire you, or do you prefer to remain in the background, doing a good job but out of the spotlight?

What I want you to think about right now are the qualities of your dream job, not so much the particulars. Whether you import coffee beans or sell designer shoes isn't the focus right now—it's how you'd like to *feel* about your job and how you'd like others to

view you. **Spend some time now writing out a fantasy job description.** Remember, don't let any perceived barriers influence what you write. Pretend anything is possible.

_____

_____

_____

_____

_____

_____

_____

_____

_____

_____

Guess what? Anything IS possible!

If you can dream it, you can do it. Did that exercise give you any new ideas? Have you expanded your horizons or added any new destinations to your career journey? Fantasy does have a purpose, because it gets you to think beyond boundaries that others may have set up around you.

But now it's time for a more reality-based check-in. If you're reading this book, you've probably already identified at least some improvements in your job scenario that you'd like to move toward. For now, limit your thinking to opportunities you know (or hope) exist where you currently work. If you aren't aware of the career paths that may be available to you, then start with defining the job growth paths in your organization and company. **List as many job advancements as you can imagine making in the next five years or so.** Be specific—say:

★ Assistant Editor; Junior Editor; Acquiring Book Editor

★ Administrative Assistant; Junior Buyer; Deputy Manager

★ Lead Technician; Shift Supervisor; Assistant to the Manager

_____

_____

_____

_____

_____

_____

These are your career goals based on what you currently know about opportunities within your organization. You may well revise this after you get further along in your career plan.

What if you just don't know what you want to do?

Larry was one of my group leaders who worked at the receiving dock. Larry is extremely bright, but his work experience was very narrow and he didn't have any higher education. When I talked with Larry we wrote out a development plan with his manager to get him into college, and we started moving him to other jobs across the facility to give him broader experience and visibility with other managers. Larry moved to our documentation group in our Product Assurance Division. He continued to move around taking on special assignments, broadening his experience base, and as a result he was promoted to supervisor. From then on he continued to move from one supervisor position to another to increase his technical knowledge.

Larry kept moving up and was promoted to a senior manager position and then finally to the Deputy Resident Director position. Back when he was stuck on the loading dock, Larry had no vision of himself as a true leader or an executive. He really didn't have any idea what the opportunities were for him within the company. **But moving from one job to the next helped him find his passion.**

So if that's your story too, keep trying new things—you'll find out what you like and don't like. If in the end if you have a job that feeds your passion, you will find both job satisfaction and life satisfaction.

Take your first steps toward a more fulfilling career
1. MEET
Make an official appointment with your immediate supervisor to discuss your career development. Your manager has a very key role in your development. It's your manager who decides your assignments, opportunities, training, classes, tuition

reimbursements and much more. Talking with your manager is essential to getting the development you need to reach your potential.

Don't just drop in on him and hope he can spare a few minutes. This is a landmark moment when you take charge of your own destiny, so you should both allow ample time for this meeting. Besides, you want to be well-prepared for this event.

Prime Pothole

One of the most common mistakes in employee advancement is failing to tell your boss you want to be developed and to what extent. If your management doesn't *know* you want to be developed or promoted, many times they won't single you out for help. I've seen numerous people who just assumed that if they did an outstanding job they would get promoted and advance in responsibility. **Never assume your supervisors know what you want—tell them!**

Start down the road to a great career by doing the self-assessment steps throughout the earlier sections of this book. (If you skipped over them, now's a great time to go back and fill those in.) Be prepared to go over your experience with your manager at your first meeting. **The most common mistakes employees make are:**

1. Thinking your manager knows your career goals.

2. Thinking your manager is totally familiar with your past experience.

3. Thinking you are already qualified for a promotion.

4. Thinking your manager is responsible for your career performance.

5. Thinking the only development opportunities are at your current job.

6. Thinking the only time for feedback is at performance appraisal time.

7. Thinking your boss will think of you first when special assignments are available.

2. DISCUSS

Have a clear, written agenda for what you want to discuss. This might include:

✔ Begin by letting your boss know that you *want* guidance and assistance in becoming a more valuable employee.

✔ Review your performance while working under this supervisor.

✔ Examine the kinds of assignments you've been given.

✔ Remind him of the special value you bring to the job.

✔ Bring an updated resume with your education and training history.

✔ Be prepared to talk about your career goals.

✔ Be prepared to discuss if your career desires are toward management responsibility or technical growth. Many companies have both management and technical advancement paths, so be clear which one you want to be on.

✔ Go over your organization charts to identify jobs you would be interested in growing toward and filling in the future. Be specific. Ask about each job and what is required for that position.

✔ It's also important to have your manager identify any additional positions she feels you should work toward. Sometimes your boss is better at seeing your potential then you are. Many people sell themselves short when it comes to job

growth and possibilities. Try not to let fear hold you back from stretching to your maximum career growth.

✔ Be sure to sincerely thank your boss for her time and help—in proportion to her level of interest. If it seems like she's ready to really go all out on your behalf, then by all means, let her know you really appreciate her help.

Be prepared to answer the following questions when you meet with your manager:

1. Why are you there?

2. What career are you interested in? If you don't know, ask your manager what she thinks your talents would indicate as a possible career path.

3. What is your current education? Be prepared with your degree information or your tuition reimbursement plan (if your company has one).

4. What training are you looking for? Technical, leadership, interpersonal, communication, presentation skills, etc.

5. What does it cost?

Be prepared to ask:

1. Ask who she thinks could act as a mentor for you. (More on this later.)

2. Ask to meet again for feedback and help in creating your development plan.

Sometimes people go into a first meeting with their supervisor all excited to begin this process, confident in their abilities and stoked about their future. But instead of getting the support they expected, they get a different reaction entirely. If you're prepared for a range of reactions, then this doesn't have to throw you for a loop. Remember, it's your supervisor's perspective you're asking for, so try and be open minded about their response. You may think you're already qualified for a particular position until it's explained to you why you're not. **Use that input to make course corrections, then the next time that type of position opens up, you *will* be qualified.**

Kristy is a good example of this. She's well educated and extremely talented. I gave her a copy of the workbook, and after reading through it she felt like she was already qualified to be a manager. Because of that **she didn't think she needed to go through the career gap analysis process.** Kristy kept searching for jobs and not getting hired, then moving laterally to other positions. She didn't really have a development plan for her career. After five years of making no real progress, she finally admitted she needed to go through the process as I outlined it. Initially she'd balked at doing it, because it was a lot of work. But after wasting five years because she didn't have a good strategy, she's finally on track for success. **While this workbook can feel daunting, I encourage you to keep at it—you are worth it!**

3. THINK AHEAD

Research your possible next position(s)

The best place to start is with the Manager of the position of interest. Don't be afraid to tell that person you're interested in either being developed for it or actually filling it now. Identify specific job responsibilities, the job scope and qualifications required. Many times the Human Resources department can supply you with complete job descriptions, which include requirements and prerequisites for each position. See if you can chat casually with someone in that position now.

4. GO UP A NOTCH

Also make an appointment to talk to your supervisor's boss—especially if your immediate supervisor seemed less than enthusiastic. Sometimes insecure managers worry that people under them are angling for *their* jobs and use that excuse to impede someone's progress. Don't do this in any secretive way—you don't want anyone in your office to think you're plotting behind their back. Simply announce at the end of your first meeting with your supervisor that

you're also going run these ideas by Mr. So-and-so for his input. You'll notice I didn't say to *ask* if you could do this, I said to announce that you *are* going to do this. Smile, be friendly yet assertive, and make the appointment. If your supervisor has been helpful to you so far, then by all means let her boss know that. Not in a suck-uppy kind of way, but just as a statement of fact. This can start a circle of gratitude that comes back to you over and over in many beneficial ways. **There are many reasons to have this meeting, too.**

You want to become known to higher level managers, as they're often the ones on the decision making panels. In addition, you're going to need mentors, and this is often where you can identify them, among people in your company who are already successful.

CHECKLIST

____ 1. Go through the value exercises and write your Value Statement.

____ 2. Write out your fantasy job description.

____ 3. List your possible job advancement arc for the next five years.

____ 4. Update your resume (see Appendix for resources regarding this)

____ 5. Make an appointment with your supervisor and be prepared for it.

____ 6. Come away from the meeting with your next job options.

____ 7. Do further research on those options.

____ 8. Also meet with your supervisor's boss.

CHAPTER THREE
Collecting Maps and Guides

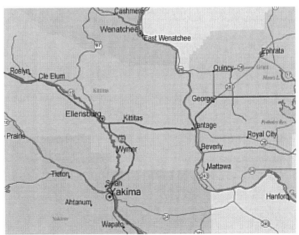

Be Coachable

As you plan your new career options, this is one of the most important qualities you can aim for. **One of the most desired characteristics managers look for in an employee is a coachable attitude.** When someone is coachable, supervisors feel their time and energy is worth investing in that person. One of the first reasons I hear from managers who have given up on an employee is they are NOT coachable. A wonderful example of a coachable employee was Sue. She was an excellent individual performer, and as a result, she was promoted to a supervisor. She thought if she used those same individual strengths that she'd succeed as a supervisor.

Unfortunately for Sue, the skills were not all the same. New skills were needed. This is true for many people who change jobs; they find different skills sets are needed. So how did she find this out? Sue came to my office one day and asked for feedback. To her surprise, I told her she was not delegating and was doing all the work herself. Her group was producing perfect products, but the employees she supervised were not being developed and grown. Sue's perfectionist streak and heavy-handed control was causing her team to stagnate.

So Sue went back and started delegating and giving the coaching needed to bring her team's skills up to the level they needed to be at. This process of Sue asking and listening for feedback on her own performance continued, and Sue kept on growing into an exceptional leader.

Unfortunately, I've also seen the opposite attitude in people. I had a very talented man working for me but he was not willing to change; Gerald thought he knew more than everyone around him. He was unwilling to alter his behavior and eventually stagnated in his upward progression, even though he was talented enough to get to the next level. He had numerous bosses and peers who tried to coach him without success. Some people just don't know how to hear feedback as anything but harsh criticism, and sadly, they often see coaching as a punishment.

What do you do if you make a BIG mistake, something that might be seen as career ending? I remember Jen, a young woman who was caught roller skating in the halls at work. She thought it was faster to get around in order to get her job done. Unfortunately management did not look favorably on her and felt she was totally immature. Taking into consideration other signs as well, her manager was heading down a path to terminate her. I asked him to give me the chance to coach her, since Jen did have a lot of talent. So I sat her down and told her how management was feeling about her roller skating and overall professionalism. I said she'd have to overtly demonstrate she could take feedback and change. Jen needed to express her repentance.

> **Acknowledging your mistakes with regret for making them is one of the strongest expressions of being coachable.**

Jen eventually showed management she was sorry, changed her ways immediately and went on to become a valued employee.

So how about you—are you coachable?

According to a 2005 study of over 5,000 managers by Leadership IQ, a global leadership training company, "46 percent of newly-hired employees will fail within the first 18 months." The biggest reason why new hires fail is that **26% are not coachable**—they are unable to accept and implement feedback from anyone. So how can you stay out of that group? **Circle any items you need to work on.**

The aspects of being coachable include:

★ asking for feedback

★ listening to the feedback

★ accepting input as positive information more than criticism

★ seeing coaching as a professional experience rather than a personal one

★ remainig upbeat in the process

★ willingness to grow and change

★ accepting responsibility for your actions and expressing regret over mistakes

★ demonstrating course corrections if needed

★ giving feedback to your coach— which may be gratitude or simply letting her know which techniques you found most effective and helpful

Meet with map makers

Don't be afraid to ask for coaching. You do *not* want to be that guy who bumbles along the wrong highways, makes wrong turns, can't or won't read a map—and above all-refuses to ask for directions. Midway through my career I moved back to the Structures Manufacturing Manager position. When I returned, Robby was a peer working for Bill, our Division Manager. Robby was really struggling to understand exactly what Bill expected of him. They had difficulty in meetings and overall communication problems. Robby asked me for coaching with a goal to get better at working for Bill.

We agreed to meet for ten minutes after each meeting, when I shared with Robby what I saw go awry and made suggestions about how to do it better next time. Ironically, the two men often agreed on things, they just didn't realize it because their communication styles were so different. **Thanks to our sessions, Robby improved significantly and became one of Bill's strongest managers.** But the key is, Robby identified the problem and sought coaching for it—he didn't expect his boss to try and fix their problem—he accepted responsibility for his own performance.

There is no shame in needing or asking for coaching. **Think of coaches as map makers who can show you exactly what steps you need to take next to get where you need to go.** Everyone can benefit from it. Even high-earning professional athletes continue to pay professional coaches to keep them performing at their best. However, the more invested you are in your job, the more you may be prone to experience feedback personally, to feel a sting when you're corrected on something. This is human nature, but the more you can separate the two, the better off you'll be. Very few feedback situations are genuinely about someone's character. Just because your boss tells you that you need to learn how to be a more effective trainer, doesn't mean she thinks less of you as a person. **Learning to distinguish between professional and personal comments will help you mature as a leader.**

Coaching can come from everyone around you. Be open to your boss, peers in other departments, co-workers on your own team, subordinates, colleagues at other companies, acquaintances from business groups, friends, family and even your spouse. It can also come from other sources. If you're really serious about self-improvement (and especially if you don't feel you have a lot of good coaches around you) be sure to consider other recourses, like the ones listed below. **Circle any that you think you'd like to investigate further.**

Librarians are great at showing you resources you'd never find on your own

Online blogs about business and management

Read trade magazines

Read books on being a more effective employee and/or manager—you're reading this one, aren't you?

Join industry groups and network within them

Attend local business groups, such as Soroptimists, Kiwanis, Chamber of Commerce, etc. to meet and network with peers in other industries. This is especially key if you're thinking about switching jobs or careers entirely.

> **Coaching is a two-way street, so do let the people who help you know how *they're* doing, and how they can be even more useful.** If someone gives you a tip that really changes your perspective on something, by all means tell them. Knowing your coaching is appreciated makes a coach want to give even more.

In addition to coaching, you'll need mentors

Let me clear about the difference. Coaching can happen informally at any time during your day. It can take just a few seconds or it can be a more formal session with a supervisor. Coaching addresses your skills and performance in specific ways and aims to resolve perceived problems or skills you may lack. **Coaching is always an opportunity for you to grow as an employee and to demonstrate the good qualities of your temperament and personality**—remember those from the last chapter? This is not the time to be irritable or moody. This is the time to be cooperative, receptive and enthusiastic. You *want* your supervisor to pay attention to you, to single you out for guidance. This is a good thing.

Mentors are something else entirely. **Mentors are the secret resource that can make all the difference in your career journey;** they are key elements in your career development process. Think of them as experienced guides who know all the routes and shortcuts. While a mentor may occasionally offer you coaching on things they think will help you in your career path, that isn't their primary function.

Mentors in my life

Actually, they can serve many valuable purposes over the entire course of your career journey. To illustrate that, I'm going to share my own career path with you and how mentors made all the difference for me.

Mentors encourage you to start new jobs

Without having mentors in my career, my life would have unfolded on a drastically different path. The path I thought I was on was to get a good paying job and do it well for the rest of my life. My father was grocery checker, and I just saw myself having some sort of job much like his. While still in school, I didn't even know there was such a thing as a career. I worked at K-Mart when I first got out of high school. No one in my family had gone to college, so it wasn't something I'd even aimed for.

Then a friend of mine got a job at a semiconductor company and told me I could make $2.20 an hour if I moved to that company doing semiconductor manufacturing. I was ecstatic having the opportunity to work at a good paying job with medical benefits. I thought things were going extremely well until John, my immediate boss was laid off. Then destiny intervened on my behalf.

My former boss went to work for a major defense contractor, and soon after he called me and said I should apply there, too. So I filled out the application and was called for an interview. Because semiconductor work was so new at that time, my two years of experience at Raytheon was highly sought after. **I guess you can say that's when I was first mentored, because John encouraged me to move to a new job.** And that company is where I stayed for the rest of my career.

Mentors inspire you to get more education

I took on my new job with gusto and energy. I hungered to learn everything I could in manufacturing the micro-electronics that we were building for a major defense product. This is when I met Pearl. She was my supervisor and became a lifelong mentor and friend. Pearl had an excellent knowledge of the company and what was needed to succeed. She was the first one to tell me to start college. I was surprised, since college was not something I'd planned to do, and besides—I hated school! But some inner urge for self-improvement won out, and I enrolled the next semester. I loved electronics, so I started working on an Electrical Engineering degree at a junior college.

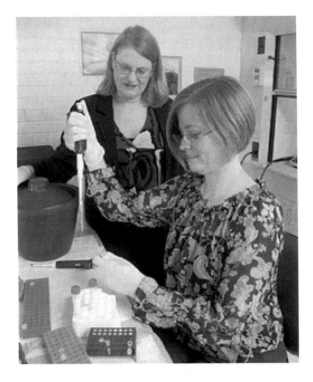

Mentors watch for opportunities and encourage stretching

At my two year mark there was a job opening for a scheduler. Pearl came to me again and asked if I was going to apply. I'd learned all the processing steps for building micro-electronic hybrids, so doing the scheduling would be a natural growth opportunity. She was mentoring me by watching for opportunities and encouraging me to stretch and get over my fear of trying something new. Sure enough, I was selected for the scheduler job, which started me on the route toward more administrative work—something I never would have guessed I'd be good at.

Mentors have faith in your abilities

The second week at my new job, Pearl called me aside and asked if I would move to swing shift as the hourly (union) lead person. I was surprised and asked her honestly if she thought I could do the job. Would my co-workers actually let someone 19 years old lead them? She had total faith in my abilities, even if I didn't. I found many times in my career that her faith in me allowed me to take on more and more challenging assignments.

And that's how growth happens, when you realize you *can* do what you didn't think you could.

Mentors network and advocate for you

A year later the Group Leader job in the manufacturing area opened up. Pearl once again encouraged me to apply. I was a natural for that job, too, since I had both performed and scheduled all the processes. This is where my leadership experience really began. Looking back now, I can see that I grew up leading throughout my youth: neighborhood groups, school and sports groups. **So when the Supervisor position opened up, I applied—but to my surprise, I was not chosen.**

This is when several women managers strategized on my behalf. When I was debriefed about the job selection, I was told that management wasn't sure if I was a successful leader. My mentors argued on my behalf that I should be moved into another

Group Leader position so that management could assess my leadership skills. Just like that, the following week I was transferred to the cable assembly department. That seemed like a minor miracle at the time and sure revealed to me the value of powerful mentors working behind the scenes.

Let me be clear though—this isn't a case of favoritism where people get their buddies or relatives promoted to cushy, well-paying jobs that they may not be qualified for. **My mentors knew—even better than I did—what my true capabilities were, and they simply pushed me to take on ever-bigger challenges so I would continue to grow.**

Mentors help you overcome fear and leverage losses

Now I landed in a whole new department, and it was very scary taking a job where I was not familiar with the hardware processes. I felt like they were all speaking a different language. I met with the manager of the department and shared my

concerns, so she met with me weekly for coaching. Notice that I didn't try and fake my way through things that were beyond me. There's nothing wrong with stating you don't understand something and asking how you can learn to do it. False arrogance will bite you in the you-know-what every time. Instead, I spent extra time reading drawings, watching training videos and reading manufacturing process documents. That helped me learn the hardware, but I still needed to demonstrate leadership skills.

This is when I learned to adopt the skills of supervisors I admired. Six months later the supervisor job opened up in the cable shop. I competed and lost, coming in second. Still not bad after only six months in the department. Soon the manager had another opening, so they gave it to me rather than repeating the selection process. At 23 I was the youngest supervisor in this very large corporation. And I never would have reached that level without the support and encouragement of so many generous mentors.

Mentoring others

That was my first formal leadership position. By then I was a strong believer in mentoring. I started meeting with all 105 employees in my department and going over their career experience and looking at what career paths might be available for them. I wanted to give back what was given to me.

At that time a lot of hiring was happening in my local company of 30,000 employees. I researched the entry-level positions and the growth potential for those career fields. I discovered that **with a small**

amount of education, many of my employees could qualify for higher hourly positions in warehousing and inspection. So I started working on development plans with each interested employee. Within one year over 100 of them were promoted to these higher positions. The downside was that created a very large challenge for me to provide efficient training for all their replacements, but it was worth it to know I'd sent so many people on to better jobs. That's when I started to think I must be onto something with a batting average like that.

Mentors develop your breadth

The following year my manager moved me to a new area that was having cost and schedule problems. This gave me an opportunity to learn about a different

customer's requirements, and to show I could turn around a poorly performing group. By the next year, my group was on schedule and under budget. Soon after that, there was an opening in the Inspection Department for a supervisor. I applied and got the job. I moved to that department to continue to increase my breath of knowledge across the large company. Over the next three years I rotated through five other supervisor positions, including auditing and finance.

You may be wondering why I changed assignments so often, especially since they didn't always signify a promotion or a raise. While many of these were lateral moves at the same level on the organizational chart, each one increased my overall knowledge of how the company worked. I was actually preparing for the next level up the corporate ladder.

It was also at this point I started mentoring employees selected as leadership development candidates. I was involved in a lot of selection panels, had begun networking with other women and began to see **the disappointing trend that women**

continually lost the selections for leadership. I was determined to get to the next level of leadership. But how I asked myself?

Mentors share selection criteria and advice about selection panels

So I began studying the selection process. Typically, three managers who were one level higher than the open position met and scored the candidates. The person with the highest score won. I asked other women managers about the criteria they were using and compared it to my experience. I noticed one interesting thing about the selection panels. Typically, the three higher level managers came from unrelated disciplines.

For the positions I was interested in, there would be one from Manufacturing, one from Product Assurance and one from Engineering. I felt I could get the vote from the two who knew me, but not the Engineering Manager. I believed if I could get exposure to the Engineering Manager, it might give me an advantage. So I started looking for job opportunities that would broaden my experience and give me

exposure to the Engineering Manager. I found a job setting up a facility in Georgia. I asked to take on setting up the engineering interface and operating procedures for how engineering would work with this new field site.

With that successful assignment, I got positive exposure to the Engineering Manager, and a year later when the Composites Manufacturing Manager position opened up I applied and won. As I expected, getting the engineering vote made the difference. I was 30 years old and was the 30th woman to be promoted to manager in a company with 30,000 employees. I was proud on two fronts: because my leadership skills were being acknowledged, but also because I knew I'd won the prestigious job by my own strategizing and careful execution. **Was it always fun to switch jobs so often? Of course not.** The easy thing to do would've been to settle into a nice supervisory job and call it a career. Lots of people do just that, and that's fine if that's your goal and your comfort level. **But I began to be driven to see just how far I could actually go.** Even I was surprised at the answer!

Mentors apply what they learn to others

I started applying my knowledge of selection panels to the development plans I was helping women create who were competing for supervisor positions. I helped them get assignments that increased both their experience and visibility. I was sought after for mentoring by employees who had worked with me in the past and by other

women and minorities in our company. **During my 35 years with the company, I successfully helped over 1,000 people advance their careers using the techniques I'm sharing in this book.**

Mentors help you develop a broad experience base

Over the next five years I held four different managerial positions in mechanical

manufacturing and one in a classified program. I found very few women mentors in the company above my manager level, so I started asking white male directors for mentoring. This was another opportunity for me to stretch, to ask the very men I used to think of as my competition to help me. As it turned out, they were especially helpful because of their extensive networks, and they were willing to share those connections with me. It was through those networks and their strong positive recommendations of my talent that doors opened for me to move into other manager jobs. Then at age 35, I was selected to become the Division Manager of Electronics Manufacturing. I had 250 employees in my division, which provided lots of mentoring opportunities for hourly workers, salaried employees and people on leadership tracks.

Mentors learn about selection panels and can leverage losses

Being a higher level manager as well a woman, meant I was asked to sit on numerous selection panels for leadership openings. It gave me an excellent perspective to understand the expectations

for leaders. It also gave me a bird's eye view of why women and minorities were NOT being selected as often as they should be. Typically, women and minorities scored second. It was clear that white men were getting more assignments in their departments, which in turn made them more qualified for promotion.

That's the point when I started advocating for women and minorities to get those assignments in order to level the playing field.

> My pushing paid off, and over the next 20 years I saw more and more women and minorities promoted to higher and higher levels. That felt really good, a genuine cap to my career as a mentor.

Mentors need to take their own advice

At age 35 I took inventory of what I wanted for the rest of my life. Clearly I enjoyed jobs that were hardware-related, but I quickly learned each new position, and I needed to be continually challenged in order to remain fully engaged. I looked across the company for jobs that fit my life goals.

Most of my family lived in the Northwest United States, so that's when I started eyeing the Resident Director position in Silverdale, Washington near Seattle. I asked the Vice President of Operations for a mentoring appointment. After sharing with him my extensive experience, I asked him what else he thought I would need to compete for that job. He felt I was already qualified, and three years later when that job opened, I applied for the position—and lost.

After meeting with the Director and VP for a debriefing, it was clear I needed what's known as remote facility experience. So I set up an appointment with my boss to find out if I could get a development assignment at one of the remote sites. I did just that and spent two months at the facility in Washington and three months at the facility in Georgia.

A few years later, when that coveted directorship opened up again, I was 39 and I won the job I'd set my sights on. Being in charge of an entire facility allowed me to create a whole new development culture at our site. We started with 197 employees and grew to 430 by the year I retired. Almost all of the employees at my facility received one or more promotions during the 15 years I was in charge.

I encourage you to learn this road map and use it for your own career and for the careers of everyone you'll mentor in the future. It has been tested and it works!

It's time to find your own bridge builders

To get started, let's just focus on a few different types of mentors, each one with a different role to play in your career development. **Your mentor can be a coach, teacher, advisor, sponsor, advocate, prodder, motivator, counselor and faultfinder.** Yes, even that last one has benefits to you, as I'll explain in a minute. Mentors can be formal or informal, and some people can mentor you without even knowing that's what they're doing. All mentors have something in common—they

help build a bridge for you to get from this side of the river to the other side—from this point on your career map to the next one.

Asking for a mentor is an important step in your long-term growth and development, but getting someone to mentor you can be difficult, because it feels scary. However, I think you'll find most people are open to mentoring and coaching people if they're asked. (It can even be a boost to their ego to be sought out in this way.)

What I've found over time is that people who are experts or leaders are very willing to mentor people. What you need to do is spend some time interviewing some of these folks and talking to them about whether they have any interest in being your mentor. Good candidates are individuals who are currently mentoring other people and are strong advocates for employee development.

I suggest selecting three people to be your different types of mentors.

Jot down any names that come to you as you read these descriptions.

CHAMPION:

This person is you main advisor or sponsor and ought to be someone who knows your office politics. **Ideally, this will be someone with positional power and influence on selection decisions.** If you work for a large company, this will likely be someone at least one level up from you. (If you're on a highly technical career path rather than a leadership track, you should instead seek a Technical Expert Mentor, someone who is highly knowledgeable in your field or discipline.) Note any names that come to mind.

workbook

_____

_____

_____

_____

_____

_____

MOTIVATOR:

This person is **someone who you can confide in about your thoughts and fears.**

She may feel more like a counselor, someone you can trust to factor your personal information into your job decisions. This mentor is someone who believes in your abilities and encourages you to grow. Another name might be your cheerleader. This person recognizes your talent, will encourage you and understands what's important to you in your life. The kinds of things this mentor can help you with are: work life balance, health issues, personal issues, religious issues, values, your passion for your job or anything else that defines you as a person. This mentor will be there for you when times are tough, when you're discouraged, when you have trouble believing in yourself. This mentor is the one who can give you the encouragement and positive input that you need. She may be higher up the corporate ladder than you are or may even be a well-placed peer, but it's someone you respect and someone who has demonstrated good judgment. She might work in a different area of your company, which is fine, or she might even be from outside your workplace, say from your church or some other organization. **What matters is that she knows you on a personal level.**

FAULTFINDER:

This is the surprising mentor, **someone who's willing to tell you exactly what you need to do to improve your job performance** on any and every level. There always seems to be someone at work who is quick to criticize and to let people know what is wrong with their ideas. This person will be frank about your weaknesses and may point out the downside of your potential job choice decisions. This mentor can be invaluable in identifying the pitfalls of any job offer, which helps in weighing which jobs you should consider going after

on your career path. By utilizing these kind of input, you are less likely to be blindsided by poor decisions which would send you toward a job that isn't a good fit. Listen to your Faultfinders and give their advice the appropriate weight in your decision making process. Your instincts may tell you that this person is NOT on your side, but in fact, you may learn the most from him or her. In truth, **faultfinders often have no idea we've figured out how to maximize their *positive* effect on our lives.** This may well be the one person on your team who everyone else avoids because he's so hyper-critical. But your big advantage is that you understand how to harness the power of this observant person—and overlook the negative packaging their advice may be wrapped in.

Now What? Now that you want them, how do you get your mentors?

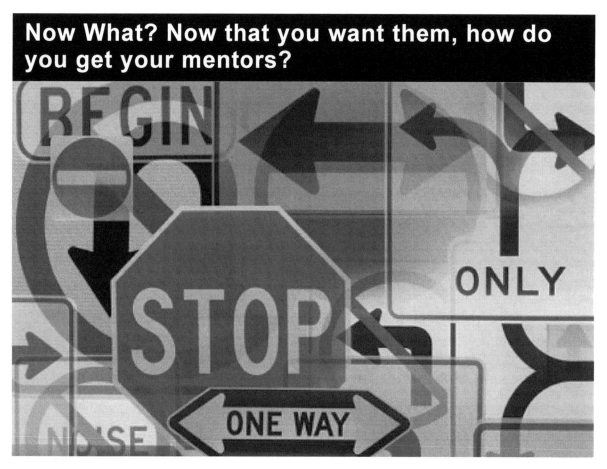

1. Start by making a list of potential mentors.

Who comes to mind when you think of someone you admire? Who has already shown an interest in you or your career? Who have you seen be helpful to others? Who have you watched steadily advance in their own career? Who seems to be well-connected in your company? To find your Champion mentor, you'll need to look at your company's organizational structure. Who are the managers above you in your leadership ladder? List the people that are one or two levels higher than your current level. If you don't know them, try to talk to someone who does know them.

2. Talk to your manager for suggestions of possible mentors.

They will know many more candidates than you will. Perhaps you'll prefer seeking a female mentor because she seems more approachable. Sit down with your supervisor and go over the names on your list and discuss what kind of mentor your boss thinks each person would be and whether that person is approachable.

3. Organize your list by the three types of mentors.

If you're missing candidates in one or more categories, continue searching by broadening your outreach. Ask more people for ideas. And if you work at a smaller company, you may even need to look beyond your own walls to find your mentors. (More on that later.)

4. Prioritize the people on your list in each group in order of their desirability.

Then go after them in that order. You might as well end up with your first picks if at all possible. Don't do this process haphazardly—this is the rest of your life we're creating here.

5. Begin with finding a mentor from the Champion group.

Make an appointment with your first choice candidate, and schedule about 30 minutes for the initial discovery phase to discuss whether they'd be willing to be your mentor. Be prepared with your resume so they can get an idea of where you're starting. Also have some ideas about where you're headed and bring along this workbook so they can see you take your career development seriously. Also, speaking with your supervisor about your plans should have prepared you for this next series of meetings. To start the meeting, be brief and concise. Tell your candidate that you're looking for a mentoring relationship to develop your career. If your potential mentor seems to need convincing, whip out your Value Statement from Chapter Two. (I told you that'd come in handy.) Ask if they'd be willing and would have time to meet with you. Be prepared to discuss how often and for how long you'd like to meet. If

they're willing, then set up your next appointment.

6. Once you've selected a Champion mentor, meet with her again.

Discuss things like how often to meet, how long he's willing to be a mentor, and what your expectations are. This person will be your primary mentor and will be the one to work with your manager on your development plan.

Remember, for those wishing to advance in a non-leadership path, you're looking for a **Technical Expert Mentor**. In this case, your manager may be the best person to select someone you can shadow and learn from. It's important to make sure this person is willing to share information. Fear of loosing a job or influence in the organization can cause people not to share their expertise.

7. Now select someone to be your Motivator mentor.

After identifying your first choice, make an appointment outside of work. Lunch or dinner often works well. Ask if they'd be willing to mentor you in making career decisions. Provide them with a copy of your resume and tell them what your immediate and long-term goals are. This can be a formal agreement or an informal relationship with someone you can confide in. If they agree to mentor you, decide how often you want to meet and schedule your next get together. Talk with this person frequently for encouragement and motivation. Discuss possible job offers and look at the personal as well as professional impact that would result from a potential new job.

8. Finally, look for your Faultfinder, someone who can help you see the other side of all the job decisions.

This person does not even have to know you see them as a mentor. Pick someone who's willing to talk about jobs with you and pass on the negative things you should consider and someone who's willing to tell you where you fall short. Have specific questions prepared that you need perspective on. To best utilize this input, always approach this person when you're feeling strong, confident and good about yourself. Remember, you may well hear things that are tough to take—but that's the point. Just don't seek this person out at the end of a rough day. Go in with your skin thick and your attitude well-adjusted ahead of time.

More tips on choosing mentors

These suggestions come from Jennifer, a graduate of my mentoring, who went on to have a very successful career. I think she offers some really good advice. I've left some space for you to note your answers to her questions.

1. Introspection.

Be sure you're ready for a mentor. Ask yourself: Why do you want a mentor? It might be to learn technical skills or knowledge. It might be to excel in your current role. Or do you need help navigating your organizational culture or preparing for future jobs?

Other questions to ask yourself are: What are you willing to invest in a mentoring relationship? (You must take the lead in the relationship, meaning that *you* are the one who's responsible for paying attention to the relationship and developing it.)

_____

_____

_____

_____

_____

_____

_____

2. Get Clarity.

You must be clear about your goals and objectives. Ask questions every chance you get and listen closely to the responses. Show you value feedback and demonstrate your commitment by applying what you've learned. Also, ask yourself: How real are your expectations? (Your company's CEO likely doesn't have the time to mentor you.) But your mentor doesn't need to be a high-level executive or someone with 25 years of experience under their belt. There are many people at all levels of the corporation who can share their knowledge and experience with you.

3. Identify your ideal mentor.

Is the mentor an executive, manager or your peer? Is she inside your organization or another? This could be an opportunity to build your network outside of your current organization—especially a good idea if you think you may want to leave your current company before too long. What specific skills does the mentor possess that you admire? My advice is don't pick your manager. That person is responsible for your performance review, developing your current skill set and for giving you timely and frequent feedback, anyway. They are sort of a freebie mentor, but they also may have a conflict-of-interest.

_____

_____

_____

_____

_____

_____

_____

4. Mentor selection criteria.

Circle ones that are important to you.
✔ Must have empathy, not sympathy
✔ Savvy about corporate politics
✔ Must be willing to contribute to the professional development of others
✔ Must be a good listener

✔ Good at generating or offering alternative views
✔ Has a good network
✔ Is respected by their peers
✔ Strategic thinker
✔ Knowledge of the business & industry
✔ Willing to provide open and honest feedback
✔ A positive attitude!

Don't give up—"NO" can be a good thing

Another former mentee, Becky, shares her story with the mentoring process. She joined our company after a 20-year career in the public sector, so she was suffering from culture shock and really need some mentoring. On top of that, the experience of being mentored was also new to her.

"The first two people I asked to mentor me turned me down. They surprised me by saying 'You can come to me anytime for mentoring on an informal basis,' which allowed me to seek additional, more formal mentors. Those mentors were less familiar with me personally and could offer a different professional perspective and assessment. I am still in awe at some of the professionals who give their personal time and energy to develop future leaders. As this book encourages, select at least three mentors. For me, I needed one to teach me corporate culture and history; one who was my encourager and pushed me to expand my horizons in both vision and logic, and most important, one who didn't sugarcoat my performance."

Becky was a quick learner and adapted well to the rather unusual culture at a major defense contractor, but there's no doubt that mentoring made all the difference for her. Here's some more great advice from her: **"YOU have to own the process.** If you don't initiate and follow through, you have no reason to complain about being overlooked or left behind. It took me awhile to embrace this methodology, as I felt like I was tooting my horn. But as a former public servant, where time spent in grade levels drove advancement, this was a whole new world."

Pay it back and pay it forward

I want to make a pitch here to everyone reading this, to at some point consider becoming a mentor yourself. Jennifer, my former mentee, has this to say about what she gets out of being a mentor:

1. It expands my own network.
2. It improves my communication and interpersonal skills.
3. It enhances my ability to provide

and receive feedback.

    4. It develops the workforce, potentially the next leader for my organization!

    5. It brings satisfaction in knowing I have an impact on someone's professional development.

      Perhaps you're already in a position to offer some guidance to others. If you can think of people you might be able to coach or mentor, even in a rudimentary way to start, note that here.

_____

_____

_____

_____

_____

_____

_____

What to do if you work in a small company or are self-employed

Just because I spent my whole career at a giant Fortune 500 corporation, doesn't mean you also have to do so in order to reap the benefits of mentoring. I'm sure my career would've looked very different without so many different job opportunities to pursue on our complex organizational chart. That said, **no matter what size company you work at, you still need mentors, and it will be well worth your time to seek them out**. Even self-employed people should consider taking this advice—perhaps those people most of all, since they tend to work in a lot of isolation without a lot of feedback.

      So where will you find them? The process is the same, the only difference is where you look for them. If you determine that you need to look beyond your current place of employment, then you really need to become a great networker. (More on that in a minute.) **Join every business-centric, professional or trade group you can find, such as:**

★ Young Entrepreneurs
★ Soroptimists (a businesswomen's group)
★ National Association of Women MBAs
★ Rotary Club
★ Kiwanis
★ Chamber of Commerce
★ Toastmasters
★ National Speakers Association
★ Others that you know of in your area:

_____

_____

_____

_____

_____

_____

Those last two are especially valuable if you need to give good presentations in your line of work, or if you aspire to. The larger your city, the more variety you'll find in these sorts of groups. Do Google searches for them, ask librarians, ask every businessperson you meet. Once you attend a meeting, ask people there where else they go to make new connections. Even if you have to drive a considerable distance a few times a month to attend meetings, give it a shot.

Be on the lookout for less conventional opportunities, too. Lynn saw an article in her small town paper about an upcoming conference for female entrepreneurs called "Do Your Dream." Sponsored by the local Soroptimists chapter, it also included a contest with cash prizes and expert mentoring. All she had to do was submit 100 words about her business idea. One week later she was standing on stage collecting her $1,000. first prize and meeting her new mentor, a local bank manager. All of which kick-started her new home-based business. You just never know where you'll find a mentor, even in a remote town of 8,00 people.

If you are geographically challenged and there are very few opportunities

where you live, then search for online groups to help you. Become a frequent visitor—and contributor—in online forums for people in your profession. Don't discount the good advice you can pick up in books, trade magazines, online courses and reading professional blogs within your industry. Start a professional Twitter account (keep it strictly business-oriented) and follow other business people. After you establish yourself and your interests, tweet out some requests for advice. I know people who've made great friends, met new clients and made long lasting relationships through social media.

> **The bottom line is, don't wander alone in the wilderness. You, too, can find yourself some wonderful guides—it might just take some extra effort.**

Networking

People operate somewhere on a spectrum between total introvert to total extrovert. Some people get their energy from being alone (introverted) or by being with others (extroverted). When I was in my 20s I believed that introverts could not change. Since I was very shy and extremely introverted I thought I would never be able to network. After each exchange with groups of people I found my energy drained. **Nonetheless, I set out to learn the skill of networking, because my career and the careers of my mentees would fail without it.** It's just that important!

When you develop relationships with your peers, with customers and with people in leadership positions, it gives you and your mentee many more doors to open for opportunities. I read books which helped, but most of all, I practiced and practiced for 30 years. You can always grow when you decide to strengthen your skills. While it's still not my favorite thing to do, I did get good at it, which is what matters. If you want to succeed, sometimes you must stretch yourself beyond your comfort zone.

For those who are extroverts, the ability to network comes easily, but that doesn't mean it's always successful. Just socializing is not networking.

Effective networking requires the skills of listening, fair exchange, negotiation and basic relationship building.

True networking is looking for opportunities to share your own knowledge and contacts to help others—not just being on the lookout for ways to advance your own career.

First you have to develop opportunities for networking. One way to get into a networking environment is by attending events and volunteering to work on events. By setting up dinners, luncheons and other gatherings, you gain the opportunity to network with people on various levels. It can also be a wonderful chance to impress a manager from another department that you might want to join someday. Through networking you are able to talk with others who may have the ability to provide opportunities, or perhaps be on selection panels in your future. Be prepared to network all across your company and with people in your personal or professional associations.

You've probably heard this great definition of luck: When preparation meets opportunity. **So make some luck for yourself.** Prepare for networking events by researching information on the people you'll meet. Read their bios in corporate publications, look them up in a company directory, research the programs or projects they're working on. Having this kind of knowledge allows you to carry on an intelligent, relevant conversation and will speak volumes about your initiative.

Then be prepared to *ask* for mentoring or volunteer for assignments. Ask for a mentoring session if the subject is broached.

If you are mentoring others, then use the opportunity to sell the skills and abilities of your mentee(s). You never know when you might have another opportunity to speak to a top executive in your organization—so don't waste it discussing sports or the weather. (Or even worse, griping about your job!)

The best example of a networker I ever met was a man named Sam. He was an extrovert and loved to network, and he was very skilled at it. He was a retired military officer, which gave him a lot in common with our customers. Sam also took every opportunity to meet with customers, coworkers and his managers. He was knowledgeable about restaurants in the area and well versed in local wines and beers. He knew how to socialize with an underlying

business purpose. Sam was also excellent at keeping in touch with people. Because he learned everything he could about people and their families, he knew how to inject a personal touch, a familiar moment that made an emotional connection between himself and his customers.

As a result, he was deeply connected to his customers and they were loyal to him, which made him very effective in selling ideas and products. Sam was an exceptional person to complement my leadership team, so I selected him for a senior staff position and later he was promoted into additional leadership assignments.

Can you name three people right now who you already know who would make good networking contacts?

_____

_____

Building Your Success Toolbox

Now I want to say a bit about what you can DO with all the newfound wisdom you'll be collecting from your mentors. We've all known people in our careers who we saw as very successful in whatever field they chose to pursue. I found over the last 35 year that taking on their qualities can increase your level of competency and strengthen your performance.

The first time I was conscious of purposely doing this was when I was 23 and working in the Electronic Cable Manufacturing shop. I worked with a supervisor named Lou who had this wonderful ability to move the women cable builders from one cable design to another. He spent time with each person when he planned to move them and explained why they needed to move across the manufacturing area. It seemed to calm the workers to have this personal exchange and understand the purpose for the change. I decided whenever I changed an employee's job assignment in the future I would use this same technique.

This process of adopting other's successful traits continued throughout my career. These may be traits you observe in your mentors, whether or not you have a formal relationships with them. **You can assume successful qualities in many ways:**

through observing others

by reading books

by taking classes

by studying different religions and cultures

by learning from mistakes, which is the best way of all

The key to taking on new qualities is they must fit your beliefs and personality.

Faking qualities is transparent to everyone around you and will cause you to be seen as inauthentic or insincere. If you come across a quality you'd like to emulate, go back to your **Value Statement from Chapter Two** and see how this new trait fits into that.

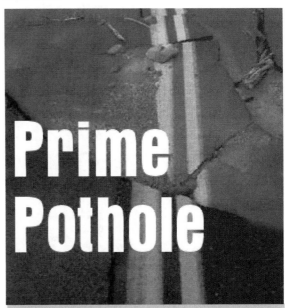

Prime Pothole

The opposite is also true. When you see people make mistakes or demonstrate bad qualities, you can also make a decision *not* to add those behaviors to your toolbox. Some of these qualities are things such as:

✔ compromising in unhealthy ways
✔ playing mind games
✔ getting caught up in office politics
✔ displaying unethical behavior
✔ bending to peer pressure

So as you go through your career, observe those around you, think about what they're doing and what qualities, skills or techniques they're using. Then make a conscious decision to either adopt or reject those qualities.

Taking Responsibility for Your Career

Okay, here's my bottom line on mentors. **There is no one better than yourself to take great interest in and control of your career.** Always remember performance is the key. There will be no path forward without performance in the job you are currently holding. All too often people measure their individual performance against the people working next to them, rather than measuring to their own personal best performance. Never slow or cut back your performance to fit in, to make your day easier, or to just get by. Your performance is your real time resume, your day-to-day job interview. That's what managers use to decide who gets job development assignments and who to promote to the next level.

After performance, the next key is initiative. You must take responsibility to advocate for yourself to get assignments, opportunities and promotions. I remember when I was a very young manager of 23, there was a 50-year-old woman working for me as a Group Leader. She was an exceptional leader and manager. I wondered why she hadn't been promoted to a manager. I asked my boss about her and told him I was surprised they hadn't promoted Dixie. I was shocked by his answer. He said he didn't think she *wanted* to be a manger. The next day I asked Dixie if that was true. She said she did want to rise to that level, so then I asked her if she ever told her bosses that. You guessed it—her answer was *no*. I found this phenomenon over and over again in my career, where talented people thought if they performed well they would get promoted. They never told their boss what they wanted to achieve.

When I told my boss that Dixie did want to be a manager, he was so surprised. With the very next opening they promoted her to manager. I saw this happen again and again, especially for women and minorities who tend not to advocate for themselves.

> So I encourage you to gain the voice you need to take responsibility for your career.

What I got out of mentoring

I have found no greater satisfaction than watching people grow and learn and to know I've invested in their future, then watch it return big dividends. **It's wonderful to believe in someone's talents and see them grow beyond their own vision for their career.** I grappled for many years about being in management versus being an individual performer. Clearly it would've been much easier to simply worry about myself than the fate of so many others. But I began to see my accomplishments resonate far beyond me through my mentees, as I observed them mentoring others, with the ensuing ripple effects that continue on even after I left the organization.

As mentors we help make people's lives better, we help them find their passion so they can enjoy their job and reach their potential. We help them balance work and home life so they can find love and fulfillment in their lives. **My deepest hope is that you'll be inspired to mentor others as you progress in your career journey.**

Checklist for Acquiring Your Mentors

__ Consider how coachable you are, (list on Page 31)
__ Note any areas of coachability you need to work on
__ Think about local sources for coaching, (list on Page 33)
__ Pursue any that you checked there
__ List possible mentors from reading descriptions beginning on Page 42
__ Talk to your manager for suggestions of possible mentors
__ Organize your list by the three types of mentors (see Page 42)
__ Prioritize people on your list in order of their desirability
__ Answer all the questions about selecting mentors (Page 46)
__ Make an appointment with your first choice candidate for your Champion
__ Prepare things to bring to first meeting
__ Meet with your new Champion and discuss logistics and your expectations
__ Select your Motivator mentor and meet outside of work
__ Identify your Faultfinder mentor(s)
__ Keep notes in this workbook about what you learn from them
__ Note anyone you might consider mentoring yourself (Page 48)
__ To look outside your company for mentoring, review list on Page 49
__ List three networking contacts (Page 50)

Notes

Notes

CHAPTER FOUR
Where Have You Been?

Passion, finding your path, and watching for the obstacle of comfort

What do you want to be when you grow up? What do you want to achieve? What's your job passion? I've met numerous employees in my career, but I want to talk about one of them who had no direction and really did not focus at all on her career. Maria was working in my warehouse, and surprisingly she already had a bachelor's degree. In addition, she'd been working at the facility for five years. I was surprised that she was still an hourly worker out in the warehouse, so I asked to talk to her and provide some mentoring.

I met with Maria and talked about what her goals were and what kinds of things she liked to do. I asked if she had a passion for leading people, leading programs or teaching people. Turns out, she did. So her manager and I started by broadening her assignments to give her more leadership assignments and to give us feedback about whether she had the people skills. What we learned is that Maria was very intelligent, capable and she demonstrated good

interpersonal and communication skills.

Another way she broadened her management abilities was to join the local chapter of the National Management Association. Within a couple years she became president of that chapter. As you can imagine, that gave her a lot of visibility with the managers who make the selections for entry-level leadership positions. So based on her being a National Management Association president, on her sitting in for leaders and getting more visibility, she was promoted to the first level of leadership.

Maria continued along in her career, but once again she lost her focus and drive to move onto the next level. Why? Because

of her comfort in her current job. **I've seen over the years that being too comfortable in your job can be a real obstacle to continued learning and growth. If you aren't at least a little uncomfortable, you're probably not stretching and growing.**

Maria was indeed comfortable in what she was doing, so every once in a while I would prod her little bit and say: "Okay, let's keep working on the gaps in your skill set and keep you moving to the next level." I asked Maria to read some leadership books and take some management classes. Once she began to grow again, she continued to move up the leadership ladder. She became the supervisor of the trainers at our facility, which was her true passion.

She really loves helping people with their education plans and working with colleges to try to help employees get their degrees. So in the end Maria found a job that she was passionate about. But she never would have gotten there without turning around and paying attention to where she'd already been and connecting that to her real passion.

Why it's important to document every step of your career

So where have you been? If you're just getting started with your work life, it may not seem like a big deal to remember details of most of the assignments you've had. But trust me, that will get tougher as the years go by. It's crucial to document everything you've done in your career, even things you can't imagine will ever matter to anyone. I promise you, some obscure one-day workshop you took can be the very thing that four years later tips the scales in your favor during a selection panel.

Trust the Voice of Experience: You cannot possibly know what aspects of your work history will matter to a potential boss in the future.

And once the opportunity to document your accomplishment has passed, it can be very difficult or even impossible to do so later.

Imagine a job interview when you're asked if you ever created and delivered power point presentations. You reply truthfully: "Sure!" Then the interviewer asks what documentation you have: scripts, slides, video, photos of you in action, memos from your superiors complimenting you on your presentation, etc. But you have none of that. Then imagine you're asked about your customer service skills, and you launch into a story about how you impressed a major client. Again, you're asked if you have documentation, such as: your agenda for the meeting, a Thank You note from the client, emails from your boss about the episode, photos of you entertaining the client, etc. Again, you have to say "No, gee, I didn't think to save any of that stuff."

So ultimately it becomes a leap of faith for the interviewer to take you at your word, knowing that many people tend to inflate their experience on resumes and in job interviews. If you're competing against someone who *does* have well-documented experience, who do you suppose will get the job? Not you.

I'll explain exactly how to do this in a moment, but first I want you to understand what I mean by documentation. **Try thinking of it as a passport that you'll create, a permit that will unlock your passage to ever greater career opportunities.** And just as you have

a real travel passport stamped at each new country you visit, at each new stop along your career, you'll add to your documentation files.

Your passport could take many forms, and to some extent will be determined by the sort of work you do. **If you create**

oversized spreadsheets or mechanical drawings or other types of designs, then you'll probably want to have a true portfolio that can contain actual examples of your work. This type of portfolio looks like a large zippered carrying case. You'll find one at art supply stores, some stationary stores and online. It can be of any size, but should be big enough to hold your largest item and display it nicely. On the other hand, if you're in administration or management and most of your documentation is on 8 1/2" X 11" sheets of paper, then a nice three-ring binder or a small zippered portfolio may be ideal. **This is something you will keep and add to for your entire working life, so select something substantial and durable.** You'll want to show it to potential employers, so also be sure it's attractive and professional looking. Who wants to hire someone who shows up with a coffee-stained, ratty manila folder of crumpled letters? You guessed it—no one!

The more complete and reflective of your experience that your passport is, the better you can compete with your peers, since most people do *not* keep good records. (In fact, just being able to document your experience can tell an interviewer a lot about you: that you care about your career, that you're organized, that you pay attention to details, that you have strong career ambitions, that you take pride in your work, and so on.) Resumes tend to be general in nature and rarely offer a potential boss what they really want to know.

Often it's just one or two things that can swing a selection in your favor.

I once had a female engineer, Rita, rotate into my group for her career development. Since I knew who her competition would be for the upcoming Manager opening, I looked at Rita's resume

and determined she should attend a Cost Account Manager class. When the selection took place the candidates were in a close pack, but in the end, the committee chose her because she had Cost Account Manager training—and more importantly, she had clearly documented it for them.

So let's use that example to look more closely at what I mean by all this.

Here's what Rita included to document her specialized training:

📌 A photocopy of the course description from the school where she took the class

📌 Her certificate of completion for the class

📌 A letter from the teacher who wrote glowingly about Rita's good work in the class

📌 A one-page summary written by Rita that listed exactly what she learned AND how she expected it could be relevant in her work. In other words, she told them exactly how she expected to apply what she learned.

📌 A sample spreadsheet that she created as part of her homework in the class

Now I can just imagine many of you groaning and thinking this sounds like so much extra work. But really, if you document each item as you go, the only extra item Rita created was the summary, which she wrote up as soon as the class ended while it was still fresh in her mind. You can see how asking a teacher for a letter two years later would not yield the same results. **Like all new ideas you implement in your life, adding to your passport needs to become a new habit, which over time will become second nature to you.** In fact, it can be fun to watch for things to add to it. We'll go into depth on this later, but I want to give you a taste of what can be done.

✔ Here are some more examples of things your career passport might contain:

✔ Test results from any assessments you've taken

✔ Flyers from workshops you attended

✔ Photos of three-dimensional projects you worked on, such as product models, tooling set-ups, signage, etc.

✔ Photos of you participating in special events, such as staffing a trade show booth or giving a presentation to a large group. (Ask a trusted colleague to discreetly snap a few photos from the back of the room.)

✔ A CD, DVD or flash drive containing videos you made or videos of you in action or power point presentations you worked on

✔ Sales charts showing the effects of your efforts, along with a letter from your superior attesting to how your involvement contributed to the increase in sales

✔ Copies of things you wrote, such as: press releases, reports, detailed memos, sales letters, customer service email replies, etc.

✔ Anything that could document how you handle customer problems, including letters you wrote to resolve them

✔ Copies of all professional licenses you hold

✔ Any feedback you've received from customers, even including simple Thank You notes or emails. A handful of those can really make a statement about your dedication to great customer service.

Then SAVE it, SAVE it…then SAVE it again!

Basically, anytime a superior says something good about you in writing, PRINT it—and save it digitally in your own source files. And by all means, keep all of this safely and securely AWAY from your workplace, NOT in your locker or in the back of a desk drawer. You'll want to work on this at home, and you should also keep backups of your digital files in MORE than one place: on multiple

A	Name	Capital	Continent	Area	Population
1	Argentina	Buenos Aires	South America	2777815	32300000
2	Bolivia	La Paz	South America	1098575	7300000
3	Brazil	Brasilia	South America	8511196	150400000
4	Canada	Ottawa	North America	9976147	26500000
5	Chile	Santiago	South America	756943	13200000
6	Colombia	Bogota	South America	1138907	33000000
7	Cuba	Havana	North America	114524	10600000
8	Ecuador	Quito	South America	455502	10600000
9	El Salvador	San Salvador	North America	20865	5300000
10	Guyana	Georgetown	South America	214969	800000
11	Jamaica	Kingston	North America	11424	2500000
12	Mexico	Mexico City	North America	1967180	88600000
13	Nicaragua	Managua	North America	139000	3900000
14	Paraguay	Asuncion	South America	406576	4660000
15	Peru	Lima	South America	1285215	21600000
16	United States of America	Washington	North America	9363130	249200000
17	Uruguay	Montevideo	South America	176140	3002000
18	Venezuela	Caracas	South America	912047	19700000

computers if you have them, on a CD or flash drive, and or on a cloud-based backup system. We've all had computer disasters, so don't trust your life's work to one storage location.

Good documentation has other benefits

Let me tell you about Laura, a master at creative documentation. After relocating to a new city, she was still unemployed when she spotted an ad for her dream job in the Sunday paper. The job was for a Jill-of-all-trades assistant to a Literary Agent. As an aspiring writer herself, Laura was ecstatic to think she might get the opportunity to learn all about book publishing from that perspective. She imagined in that large city there would be lots of competition for such a plum job, so she decided to go all out to try and get it.

First she organized her resume in a wildly creative way: as an issue of the weekly trade magazine, *Publisher's Weekly*.

She wrote a news article about her own hiring at the Literary Agency, which allowed her to include her bio. She wrote other mock articles that showcased her various skills and experience. Then she created bestseller lists that only featured clients of the agency in question. The mocked up book reviews contained raves from her previous employers. Everything in the magazine was designed to show that because of her related experience in magazine publishing, Laura was an ideal candidate for this job.

Laura went one step further and laid out the magazine in a desktop publishing program, printed it out and assembled it to look identical to the real thing. As you might imagine, she got an immediate interview. **Taking no chances, she made sure to bring actual samples of everything she'd ever done that might be relevant to the job.** As Laura shared these with her prospective boss, she could see it was going well, which increased her own enthusiasm.

At the end of the interview, Laura learned that over 300 people had applied for the job. Not only was she hired on the spot, here's what she was told: "This is the most impressive resume and presentation I've ever seen, so much so that I can't hire you as my assistant. I'm going to have to make you my partner." So not only did Laura get the job (and a hefty raise from the stated salary) she also started to earn commissions and other benefits of being a partner in the business. **All because she knew how to present her experience in a way that displayed her talents to her maximum advantage.**

And here's a fun kicker to this story—several years later, during an office remodel, Laura came across the file of applications for the job she'd won. Curious, she leafed through the resumes of the 300+ people she'd beat out. She was shocked to realize there were several people with much better experience than her own, people who—on paper at least—appeared even better suited to the position than she had been. Some of them never even got an interview though, because Laura made such an outstanding presentation that she secured the prize position on the spot.

Now admittedly, this is an extreme example, but I share it to get you thinking beyond the usual 8 1/2" X 11" box that most people fit their lives into. Great documentation can have ripple effects, too. Perhaps you aren't the best candidate for a particular job, so you don't get that one. However, because you made such a sterling impression on the interviewer, she *wanted* to help find you the perfect job, and she made sure you heard about another opening that suited you even better. **Managers have no trouble recognizing outstanding employees when they make it easy for them to do so**, and managers will pass you along to someone else if they think they can make a good match for you.

You may be surprised that even doing this part of the process can provide clarity, perspective and new ideas for jobs you'd like to try and momentum to continue this journey. Having your career passport up to date also means you're prepared to apply for jobs at a moment's notice, which can be a huge advantage when there are lots of applicants. Few managers can afford to interview dozens of people for an opening,

so the first person who shows up with impressive experience is going to rise to the top of their list. It all boils down to this: **do your best work and do an even better job of documenting it**, and you'll leap to the head of the line for promotions.

You may be more impressive than you thought

Imelda is a legal secretary who's a perfect example of that. She'd convinced herself that she would never advance very far because she'd lost sight of what she already *had* accomplished in her ten years on the job. Once Imelda listed all her skills (even ones not currently being used) she grew in self-confidence and was able to envision taking on more responsibility and aiming higher. Taking an approach she knew lawyers would understand, she organized her experience by cases she'd worked on. That jogged her memory and allowed her to recall the unusual aspects of each case which had required something new from her each time. **Once she began to articulate the wide variety of tasks she does over the course of a year, she soon realized just how great an employee she was.** In the rush of day-to-day life at a busy law firm, Imelda didn't often get the kind of feedback that would have reminded her how valued she was. After doing this process, she went from feeling stuck to being optimistic and recharged, so she dared to apply for a job she hadn't felt qualified to do. And the minute her supervisor realized the full breadth of her experience, Imelda was on her way to Promotion City.

Being seen from your last job

While I was Division Manager over Electronics Manufacturing, there was an opening for the Mechanical Division

Manager position. I was interested to see if they were going to consider Pearl for the job. I met with my boss and asked him whether he had considered letting Pearl compete for the job. He was surprised, because Pearl was currently his Manufacturing Finance Manager. Since I knew Pearl's work experience, I let him know she had two technical degrees and had run numerous manufacturing areas as well as Manufacturing Engineering in her past. He was not aware of her background, since he'd only worked with her in her current job. I made a note to watch for this in the future and have been surprised a few times myself when I've asked for employee work history folders and read them from cover to cover.

The moral of this story is, without boasting or being obnoxious, **it never hurts to make your colleagues and supervisors aware of the full range of your work experience**.

Try and ease it into conversations when it's relevant. Say you're working on a big presentation, and no one on your team seems to be sure which software would be best to use. If you've done this before, don't be shy and offer to guide the team: "When I worked for Acme Corporation we had a similar situation, and I learned how to use GoToMeeting webinar software to conduct a live, cross-country meeting online. I'd be happy to show you how it works."

Not only will your team be grateful, your boss is sure to notice. And of course, don't forget to document as many aspects of the project as you can.

In this case, you could do lots of interesting things:

★ Print out some page(s) from the GoToMeeting website that detail what the service does

★ Save a copy of the meeting agenda

★ Take screenshots on your computer that actually show how many people participated and what cities they called in from. You could even show how a webinar works, as in the sample below.

★ Print copies of slides you prepared ahead of time to share during the meeting

★ You can even record an entire webinar, either in audio or video, which might be impressive if you were the moderator or an active participant in it

★ Near the end of the webinar, you might even ASK for feedback from all attendees to evaluate the usefulness of the medium for future meetings. (They don't have to know that you also want the feedback for your own portfolio!)

Get into the habit of asking yourself near the end of every work day:

What special or unusual thing did I do today that I could document for my passport?

Then stay an extra few minutes to do whatever it takes to at least start the documentation process. Just cementing this

one skill into your work life can change your entire career for the better.

Creating the passport to your future

By now, I imagine you're starting to understand the kinds of things you'll want to document from your own career. I'm going to make it even easier, by guiding you through the process step by step and giving you worksheets to fill out. In this next section, you'll learn:

✔ how your passport might be used and who could potentially see it

✔ how it's used with your resume and how it differs

✔ how your passport should be expanded beyond work

✔ how to create it

✔ what level of detail is needed

✔ what kinds of documentation to seek

✔ alternative forms of documentation

✔ what to do if you lack documentation

✔ dealing with uncooperative gatekeepers

✔ what to do if even this part of the process feels overwhelming (which it sure could for someone who's already had a long career)

There—don't you feel better already? So let's get started.

How your passport might be used and who could potentially see it

I imagine that the vast majority of the time, the documentation of your work history and skills will be used for your benefit. After all, YOU control it, you safeguard it and you decide who to give to.

On the other hand, some managers may ask you to leave your career passport with them so it can be shown to other people on a selection panel or other managers who might be interested in you. That seems fine, too.

However, do realize that once it leaves your possession, you can't be sure who else is going to review it. I don't want to make you paranoid, but if you work in a highly competitive environment, some caution may be wise. I can imagine a scenario wherein a manager's assistant is attracted by the impressive looking portfolio (or has even heard her boss raving about it) and she peeks at it when he's away. Then she might realize you're angling for a job that her pal also wants, so she shows your portfolio to her, too. Well you can spin out all sorts of possibilities from that.

I truly hope you do NOT work in an environment where colleagues sabotage one another—I hope you work where you don't have to give this a second thought. But on

the off chance that you do need to consider this, think what it would mean to you if your passport suddenly "disappeared." For one thing, I sure hope you have digital copies of everything safely stored so you can recreate it. However, if your passport contains one-of-a-kind drawings or models that can't be recreated, then you might want to think twice about leaving those items in it if you're asked to give it to someone. You can always remove those particular items and say: "I never let these out of my sight—I'd be happy to review them with anyone, but they're irreplaceable."

To end with a happier scenario, you might also envision your carefully assembled portfolio being passed up the food chain from supervisor to manager to high level executives—and each one being impressed and making note of your name for future reference.

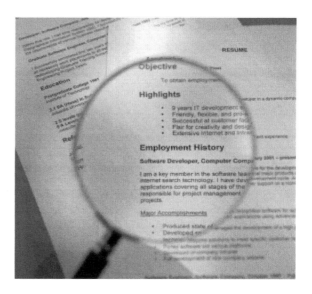

> **The next thing you know, you're being offered all sorts of leadership development opportunities and being groomed for great things. All because you made something permanent, portable and positive to promote your own career.**

How your passport is used with your resume and how it differs

These two things work as a team to give a comprehensive view of who you are and what you've been doing with your work life. Your resume is a comprehensive listing of your education and job history, as well as a detailed list of your skills. Keep in mind that different industries have widely varying standards about what they like to see in resumes and how they want them presented. **Coaching you on how to put together a great resume is beyond the scope of this book, but I do urge you to research the best practices in your field.** As a rule of thumb, the more creative your job description is, the more leeway you have in how you represent yourself. A graphic designer can get away with having a colorful, illustrated resume, while a bank teller probably could not.

Your career passport is an extension of your resume, in that it demonstrates many if not most of the claims you make. This is the tangible proof that you know how to create complex and attractive excel spreadsheets and pie charts. This is the real evidence that you know the difference between SEO and ISP. This is the documentation of all of your hard-earned

skills and abilities. **It ought to impress everyone who sees it, and that includes you!** I doubt that you—or anyone—ever works in a job where enough praise and feedback is given. Sadly, many managers only take notice of employees when they need correction, and they fail to support and appreciate the ones who *are* doing a good job. In those situations it's easy for your self-confidence to erode over time and to feel like you've stagnated in your job. That's why putting together your passport can be a real boost, not just to your ego, but to your whole outlook.

Why create a passport in addition to a resume?

Yes, it's extra effort outside of work. But as the commercial says—you're worth

it—and your future earning capacity and job satisfaction is surely worth it. Most organizations have general job descriptions. What I've seen in practice is the top performers are given additional assignments and growth opportunities beyond their job description.

Documenting this in detail gives you an advantage over your peers with the same job description. You may have worked for a manager who sees you're talented and gives you lots of assignments that are actually outside your job classification. But if you don't document all that work, there's no way that a hiring manager you're trying to impress will know you have that extra experience.

Customizing your resume for each new job opening

It's important to make sure that you keep notes so when it's time to update your resume for a job opening, you can customize it just for that job opening. How? By emphasizing your most relevant experiences and skills and de-emphasizing or even deleting ones that won't be of interest. You can glean from your history the key elements you want to make sure are in your resume in order to compete for that particular job. The level of detail that's needed depends on who will be reading your resume and what level you're applying for in your organization.

When you're just starting out your career, you want to build a resume with everything you possibly can. Your resume can become shorter the longer you're in an

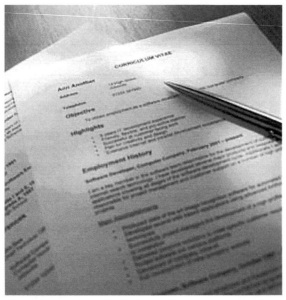

organization (and especially when the person reading your resume knows you).

Typically people who make hiring decisions don't verify details unless they seem really far-fetched. However, you don't want to say you have some experience if you really don't, because when it comes to *doing* the new job you won't be able to perform. And that is NOT the kind of information you want in your employee records!

How your passport could be expanded beyond work

Employers also care about the rest of your life experience. They need to know what kind of person you are. Which is why **your passport should also contain information about other relevant activities outside your work life.** Here are some examples of that:

📍 You volunteer at your local food bank and are in charge of the inventory of over 5,000 items from over 75 suppliers

📍 As a woman who works in a male-centric field, you're often asked to speak to college women about your experiences to encourage more women to enter your industry

📍 You volunteer at your local library and teach literacy once a week

📍 Over the years in your spare time you've built six different websites for friends and family who were starting businesses

You run your own small blog about finding local bargains

You lead nature walks for your local Audubon Society on weekends

You teach CPR at your local YWCA

You help plan parties and special events for the Boys & Girls Club

Jet-propelled Tip:

(Yes, this really is a jet-propelled bicycle. I chose it to symbolize how something mundane could accelerate your career in a big way.) What do all of the above activities have in common? **They all demonstrate portable skills you might be able to use in a job.** Beyond that, they also show what kind of person you are: helpful, generous, thoughtful, etc.

So how would you document some of those? Easy. **Have someone take pictures of you leading your nature walks and print those at the top of a page where you explain what *you* learn from the**

experience. Such as:
- ease with public speaking
- research skills as you study local and migratory birds
- organizational skills as you integrate facts into your talks
- promotional writing, since you make flyers about your talks and send press releases to local papers
- leadership skills, as you manage unwieldy groups of people and keep them on task
- how to improvise, when storms impact your walks

There are probably many others, but you get the point. Add to that the flyers you create, any agendas or talk notes you write, and by all means, a note from a supervisor applauding your contributions.

DO NOT BE AFRAID TO TELL SOMEONE EXACTLY WHAT SORT OF REFERENCE YOU NEED.

I shouted that at you because that's how important it is. You could say: "I love leading these nature walks for you, and I've learned so many skills during the year I've been doing them. Now I'd like to let my employer know what I've been up to here. Would you be willing to write a reference I can use that details my activities for the Audubon Society?"

When asked what you mean by

"details" TELL the nice people! Say: "I'd love it if you would comment on my ability to handle large groups, how you think I do with public speaking, how well I organize materials, and so on." **Here's an insider secret: more often than not, busy leaders will simply suggest you write your own reference and they'll sign it.** (Just be sure to have it printed on official letterhead.) If you're given that opportunity, don't leave anything out.

Now imagine that you're up for a promotion where some of these traits are valued, and even though these are NOT things you get to do in your current job, because you do them in *another* venue and can document them, you still get credit for them. Suddenly giving up your Saturday mornings takes on new meaning, doesn't it?

Compass Point

Now that you can see how outside activities might advance your career, you can also reverse engineer the process. Let's say you're a bit of a ham, someone who's never been shy in front of groups. Let's also say you'd love a job where you do training or any situation that puts you in front of an audience. However, there aren't any opportunities to do that where you now

work. No problem. Find a volunteer situation (such as leading the nature walks) where you can excel at those activities. Spend a year or so honing your skills in that arena. Remember to document everything. Then, start looking for a new job that has that sort of interactivity and use your volunteer experience to land the new job. While this approach may seem a bit more self-centered and less altruistic than simply volunteering for a good cause, there's nothing wrong with this approach. Just think of it as multi-tasking and great time management.

How to create your career passport

By now you may have a good idea how to proceed, but if you want the process broken down further, use the worksheet on the next page. (There are finished examples on Pages 195-7.) Whether or not you decide to include this form in your documentation, you may find it useful to organize your materials. **What follows are elaborations on the various headings on the worksheet.**

DEPARTMENT: If you work at a small company, then this will be irrelevant. Otherwise, note which department you worked in. If you moved among several, then fill out each experience separately. Examples are: Product Assurance, Human Resources, Finance, Manufacturing, Engineering, etc.

POSITION: What was your job function? Was it: Individual Contributor, Project Leader, Manager, Director, Engineer, Mechanic, Inspector, etc.

SPECIALIZATION: What was your main activity? Examples are: audits, budgets, material review board, inspector, subcontracts

EDUCATION: List ALL of your training: AA, BA, BS, MA, MS, MBA, PHD degrees, company courses, seminars, specialized training

SKILLS: Be very specific and don't be afraid to have a long list here—just be fully prepared to discuss each one, and wherever possible, show documentation for each skill. They might include: leadership, mentoring, development, management, organizing, listening, networking, teamwork, change management, negotiating, stress management, technical abilities, working with difficult people.

SUCCESSES & LESSONS: This is where you note what you learned and how you applied your skills. Be ready to discuss each one with examples. They could include: developed relationships, importance of communication skills, importance of prioritizing and delegating, improved reporting skills, improved presentation skills.

CAUTION! Don't forget these steps:

✔ After putting together a comprehensive passport, spend some time improving your resume and making sure your skills, abilities, knowledge and experience are all documented in your employee folder and files in your company's Human Resources Department.

✔ Make sure you have an updated resume on file once a year.

✔ Work with your manager to make sure documentation on performance reviews or special assignment letters verify your achievements in your folder.

WORKSHEET: Mapping My Work History

DEPARTMENT

_____

_____

POSITION

_____

_____

SPECIALIZATION

_____

_____

EDUCATION

_____

_____

SKILLS

_____

_____

_____

SUCCESSES & LESSONS

_____

_____

_____

_____

_____

_____

_____

_____

_____

_____

WORKSHEET: Mapping My Work History

DEPARTMENT

_____

_____

POSITION

_____

_____

SPECIALIZATION

_____

_____

EDUCATION

_____

_____

SKILLS

_____

_____

_____

SUCCESSES & LESSONS

_____

_____

_____

_____

_____

_____

_____

_____

WORKSHEET: Mapping My Work History
DEPARTMENT

_____

_____

POSITION

_____

_____

SPECIALIZATION

_____

_____

EDUCATION

_____

_____

SKILLS

_____

_____

_____

_____

SUCCESSES & LESSONS

_____

_____

_____

_____

_____

_____

_____

_____

_____

_____

WORKSHEET: Mapping My Work History
DEPARTMENT

_____

_____

POSITION

_____

_____

SPECIALIZATION

_____

_____

EDUCATION

_____

_____

SKILLS

_____

_____

_____

SUCCESSES & LESSONS

_____

_____

_____

_____

_____

_____

_____

_____

Where to find information for your passport

In order to document your career, information can be found in several ways. Get copies of your resumes, job performance evaluations, letters of commendation, letters documenting your sit-in assignments, training records, comb your

memory and the memory of those around you. Utilize these sources to identify all the skills, knowledge and training in you've accumulated. Look at the details of your previous evaluations, because they typically outline what you did and how you did. It's important to harvest as much information as possible for this worksheet.

Another tip is: going forward, keep a journal to document what you're learning (and don't forget to put *that* skill on your list). **Keep copies of class course completions, lists of books that you've read—virtually any documentation showing anything that would reflect how you are broadening your experience base to build your career on.** When you sit

down with a manager who has a job opening, it gives them a better idea what your skill sets are.

A tendency not to brag is a deterrent to documenting a person's experience. I've coached many employees, especially women and minorities, who tended to be shy in bragging about themselves, or else they failed to document the things they should have.

This passport process forces you to display all your experience without feeling like you're bragging; it becomes a fact gathering exercise.

YOU must take full responsibility for where you land on this career journey...do you want to spend time in a meadow or a swamp? The choice is yours, and the path to follow begins here.

What kinds of documentation to seek

 There's so much room for variation here, that all I can do is make some general suggestions, so let this list spark ideas more pertinent to your specific profession. **Check all that you think apply to you:**

EDUCATION:

___ If you've attended college in the last five years, are there class assignments that might be relevant?

___ Course descriptions for any specialized class, workshops or seminars you've taken. This could be printed from a website or photocopied from a catalog.

___ Certificates or other proof of course completion

___ Notes or letters from instructors (especially good if you did outstanding work and/or did extra projects or assisted the teacher in some way)

___ Your own summaries of what you learned from the course (see Page 63)

___ Relevant examples of course work. For example, if you created a mock website for the class, be sure to preserve it before it disappears.

SKILLS:

___ Examples of your work that illustrate specific skills, such as spreadsheets, emails, photos of you repairing an engine, etc.

___ Any written feedback from supervisors that refers directly to your skills

___ Results on specialized tests, especially ones that demonstrate proficiency

___ Copies of any certifications you hold

___ Copies of any awards you received pertaining to your skills

SPECIALIZATION:

___ Anything that demonstrates your experience in a specific area, for example: meeting agendas, inventory control programs, budget memos, auditor's report (financial data can be redacted if needed)

SUCCESSES & LESSONS:

___ Write your own summaries for each important position you've held

___ More general letters of recommendation from previous supervisors

___ Any emails, memos, etc. which speak specifically to what you've learned from a particular assignment.

TIP: When a supervisor gives you a verbal compliment, especially after an important project, don't hesitate to ask if he would mind sending you an email to that effect for your file. If he was sincere, he should be willing to do that. I'm going to say it again: **Don't let modesty or shyness prevent you from documenting all the applause you get.** (And here's an added benefit: on those down days when you're feeling like the world is against you, go home, make a cup of tea and curl up with your applause file. Reading the sincere appreciation you've received over the years can be a great emotional boost.)

Alternative forms of documentation

In addition to the obvious forms already mentioned, there are many other ways you might document your accomplishments. Don't worry about how that may seem to your colleagues. Just do it! Being too self-conscious never won anyone a promotion. The nature of your profession will dictate which of these make sense for you, as well as inspire additional methods to try.

• **Audio files on CD, DVD or flash drive.** We've all heard the recorded message: *This call may be recorded for training purposes.* Well, if customer service is your niche, then allowing a prospective boss to *hear* you doing your best, could be awesome. You could get really creative and package it like a music CD, calling it Roshanda's Greatest Customer Service Hits. Do a fun cover for the case with your photo on it, even liner notes with some biographical info or lessons

you've learned about giving world class service. They're easy and cheap to have reproduced online, so you can hand them out whenever you give someone your resume. Can you say off the charts?

• **Ditto video.** If what you do is interactive or very

physical in nature (as opposed to sitting at a desk all day long) then capturing yourself in action might be of very high value. These days most phones have video capability, or get one of those tiny pocket video cameras. Even if you have to bribe a pal with a nice dinner to stay late some night to shoot the video, it could be worth it. Again, you might package it in a case with a special cover and inserts. **Or you could upload video clips to YouTube on your own secret channel that you open just for this purpose.** It's free and it's easy to mark videos as private, so that no one can see them unless you want them to. Then you would just put a link to your channel in an email or on your resume. (For convenience, if you make the link live, then even in a digital Word document, the link will be clickable.)

• **Go 3-D**. If you design, build or work on things in three dimensions, then how can you best preserve examples of what you do? Are there interim versions that would otherwise be discarded that you could keep? Are there project models that are no longer needed that you could rescue? At the very least, take photos of your work.

• **Sure beats 1,000 words**! If photos seem like the best route for you to take, think about making inexpensive albums to handout. These days, 4x6 prints are very cheap when ordered online, and it's easy to find ready-made books that will hold 20 or 30 photos. These could be a mixture of images of you at work doing your

thing, along with actual product shots or slides from presentations. Make a nice cover or title page, and you'll have something extra special to hand out that will really set you apart from all your competition.

• **Industry-specific mock-ups**. Remember the story about Laura, who made

a mock-up of her industry's trade magazine? (Page 65) How could you do something similar? Do you work in the building trades? Could you deliver your passport as a blueprint? Are you in the medical field? Could your passport take the form of a patient's chart, perhaps even contained in a snappy metal case just like the real thing? Work in an insurance office? How about writing a mock policy that "insures" you as a great employee and the best choice for the job? Sell cars? Make a mock brochure with you as the next new model in the showroom. Have a military

background? Show a map of your deployments with paragraphs about the main lessons of each one. **Beyond the novelty of the presentation format, try and find ways to use the form to also reveal the depth of your knowledge in that field.**

What else do all these approaches say about you?

That you're creative, innovative, ambitious, focused and you go after your dreams. That sounds like an ideal employee to me!

TIP: You might also keep in your passport a running list of projects you worked on and their dates in case you need to refer back to them. Why? Because when it comes time for your performance review, **you'll have proof of what you've done, should there be any dispute.** It will also come in handy as you evaluate what you enjoy about your current job—and what you don't.

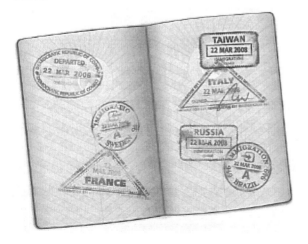

What to do if you lack documentation

Especially if you've been around more than a few blocks in your life, all of this may seem daunting if not impossible. That's why I want you to start with the worksheet on Page 76. Then at least you'll have the bones of your career on paper. Then, working backward from your current position, do the best you can to document your most recent activities.

Most of the time, what you did last month and last year are far more important than a meeting you ran a decade ago. (Of course, if you do have major career highlights in your past, do whatever you can to illustrate them in some way.)

Most of all, dedicate yourself to doing an excellent job of preserving your career from this point forward, so that five years from now, you'll look grand on paper.

Dealing with uncooperative gatekeepers

What do I mean by that? **Gatekeepers are people in any position of authority whose words or actions can impact your career.** They might work in your HR department or even be your supervisor. They may stall out on getting you important documents or fail to alert you to new opportunities. They could turn you down for education vouchers or say you can't attend a particular workshop. They might even spread lies about you. Sadly, not everyone you meet will want to help you advance in your career. There are many possible reasons for that, but all you need to know is that it's usually about *them* and their bad attitude, not about who you are. Of course it's always possible to change someone's opinion of you (especially if it's founded on misinformation). If you believe that's the case, then it may be worth giving that approach a try.

Otherwise, try hard to work around that person. **Having an influential mentor can really help here, as she can steer you in other directions and offset any negatives the gatekeeper throws at you.** If the obstinate person really seems out to sabotage you in some way, this is when documenting all your good qualities and accomplishments is crucial. As a last resort, you could take that sort of evidence and go over the gatekeeper's head to the next level and hope you find more fairness there.

This is never an easy situation, but it can be overcome. Whatever you do, don't use someone else's actions as an excuse to retreat into victimhood or dormancy in your career. If anything, use it as a spur in your side to move on to another position well away from this gatekeeper.

What to do if even this part of the process feels overwhelming

If you've made it this far in my guidebook, give yourself some applause! But if you're also dejected by what seems a lot of work, **keep reminding yourself**

what's at stake: a greatly enhanced career, far more opportunities than you can even imagine now, increased pay and benefits, more job satisfaction and so many other good things. Plus, all of these things also impact the rest of life, making it exponentially better as you achieve stability and success in your work life. Whenever you have a big project to tackle, remember this bit of strange wisdom: How do you eat an elephant? One bite at a time.

Okay, so now you know where you've been…next, we'll look at where you're going. This is going to be a fun trip.

CHAPTER FIVE

Where Are You Going?

Get out your travel brochures

You probably know how to plan a successful vacation trip: you daydream about what sort of place you'd like to go, you do some research online, maybe visit a travel agent or tourist bureau and pick up some seductive travel brochures. Then you figure out your budget, check costs for transportation, lodging and so on. Finally you crunch the numbers and weigh the activities you want to do against what things are going to cost, making your final choice of destination.

Then again, maybe you're the sort of person who throws a few clothes in a bag and heads out in your car, allowing your mood and serendipity to be your guide. For you, it's about the journey more than the destination. Both approaches to travel can be applied to your career journey, but the first one is far more likely to yield positive results.

Whether you're currently employed or not, you've probably already established your career identity and goals. For example, you may believe you're destined to be in retail management for the rest of your life. Or perhaps you're on track to become an account executive at an ad agency. Then

again, you might be feeling really stuck in a manufacturing position and have no clue how to advance beyond what's in front of your face. None of that matters right this minute.

Right now I want to encourage you to set aside everything you've ever believed about your own potential and your career path. Forget the limiting ideas others have foisted upon you. Silence your inner critic who nags you and holds you back. Instead, just relax.

I'd like you to unlock your mind to all possibilities, to see your job future as wide open as a clear blue July sky.

Because the truth is, that's exactly what your future looks like. That's the best thing about the future—it hasn't happened yet, so it's still within your power to change it. **At any moment in your life, you can always make a different choice:**

- You can choose to believe in

yourself again.

• You can push yourself to dare something new, to take a risk.

• You can decide to go back to school and get your degree.

• You can pledge to do whatever it takes to qualify for the dream job you've always wanted.

Let me tell you about Morgan. She'd always been one of those freewheeling travelers who just went where the road took her. Maps were for sissies, she believed. But after quite a few years bouncing from one dead-end job to another, she finally matured enough to realize another approach was needed—especially since she now had two

kids to support by herself. Eventually she met Jacob, who became her mentor and who gave her some goal setting books to read. It took Morgan awhile to see the value in them, but she stuck with it, and about halfway through the second book the proverbial light bulb finally lit up her brain. **One of the exercises had her think about what activities she'd enjoyed as a child.** As soon as she remembered herself playing basketball, Morgan realized what she'd always wanted to do was be involved in some sort of sport. Maybe even as a coach. In fact, she recalled playing on a company softball team in her early 20s and loving every minute of it.

That thought led her to research what additional education she'd need to become a high school phys ed teacher. Because Morgan was able to earn some life credits for her various experiences, it only took another year of classes to get her teaching certificate. And now she spends nearly every day working outside in sunny California, **deeply fulfilled knowing she's helping young girls be healthy.**

How about you? I bet it's been a long time since you daydreamed about activities you enjoyed as a child. So let's take a trip down memory lane. **Write down**  **everything you can remember that you found fun to do when you were young.** Don't try and see the career potential in it, just stay within your child's mind and look for pleasant memories, for experiences that made you feel good about yourself. What did you wish for when you blew on a dandelion seed head? How did you think your adult life would look? Who did you admire back then?

_____

_____

_____

_____

_____

_____

_____

_____

_____

_____

_____

_____

_____

_____

_____

Obviously, not every little girl who sewed doll clothes is destined to be a fashion designer, nor were your own childish visions of your future probably very realistic. But what I hope you can recapture is the naïve openness to all possibilities—that state of believing in everything.

Any surprises? Looking back on your childhood, perhaps you had a passion for playing soccer, being on the debate team, learning how to be a great chef or writing a wonderful play. Maybe a lack of encouragement caused your passion to evaporate. For some, this developed into a pattern of feeling unsupported. Perhaps you didn't know how to turn your passion into a career—or even realize that was possible. Over time, you may have learned how NOT to live your dream.

These are all clues to some of your core passions, especially ones you may have forgotten about.

Maybe you had to drop out of school, or perhaps financial pressures forced you to take jobs that weren't necessarily what you wanted to be doing. It doesn't matter why or how you ended up where you are right now. It only matters how you move forward into a career you want to thrive in.

It's never too late unless you let it be

Why do you suppose so many dreams and ideals die unfulfilled? Why do so many women slowly allow their youthful visions of what their lives could be disappear into over-scheduled reality? **Can you still see the faint outline of ambitions and desires that once excited you?** Do you remember the thrill of your first job? What happened? Life happened.

Perhaps you compromised for the sake of your family. You made adjustments to create stability in your life. Increasingly, you took the safer routes. Eventually, you may have allowed greater meaning to leach out of your life, like nutrients washed away from the soil after a hard rain.

But it's not too late for you.

Do you see any nuggets of desire that may still lie unfulfilled in your heart? Did you get a glimpse of a different you, one who may seem happier than you are now? Is it painful to confront dreams you may have let die? Your answers may already reflect an absence of possibility thinking. It all depends on what kind of life you've had and what encouragement and support you received.

Here's the good news: none of that matters anymore. As adults we make our own opportunities, and we are all given exactly the same number of hours in every day to shape our lives.

• If you didn't get the kind of education you wanted, take some night classes or get your degree online.

• If no one cheered you on or applauded your dreams, gather your mentors or start a mastermind group of like-minded people who will support each other's plans.

• Wonder how you ended up working at your county health department, when what you really wanted was a career in the media? **Why not find out if your skills are transferable** to a job at a local radio station or newspaper?

It's rarely too late to bring at least some part of an old dream to life.

Sure, no matter how many steps you practice, the ballerina boat has sailed—but you could still work at a ballet school helping young girls reach for *their* dreams and find a measure of fulfillment that way. Was medical school a goal of yours? Figure out what aspect of being a doctor appealed to you, then search for another job in the healthcare field that offers the same rewards.

For example, when her father died, Judy dropped out of college to help support her younger siblings. "Without a degree, I drifted from one unsatisfying job to another," she says, still obviously saddened by the wasted years. Confiding her old goals to a friend one day reignited her passion for medicine. "I realized it was helping patients recover—not the blood and guts of medicine—that attracted me." **Eventually Judy became a patient advocate,** someone who goes with elderly patients to all their medical appointments, takes notes, gets their prescriptions, researches their treatment options, and so on. In short, she gets the satisfaction from medicine that she had dreamed of many years earlier.

Is there some remnant of an old career dream you could revive and explore? Jot down any new ideas here:

_____

_____

_____

_____

_____

_____

_____

_____

_____

_____

_____

_____

_____

_____

_____

Go ahead...dream your biggest dreams

Remaining in this open-minded space, now I'd like you to fantasize about your dream job (without worrying about how you'd get it). Think about all the details:

- What's your work environment?

Indoors or out?

- Do you work alone or are you part of a team?
- Do you have lots of responsibility or do you want someone else to direct you?
- Are you tethered to your desk, or are you out and about, calling on clients?
- Do you prefer a quiet office or do you thrive on hubbub?
- Would you like interacting with the public or do you want to remain in the back office?
- Can you handle pressure, or do you just want to clock in and clock out on schedule?
- Like working with numbers? Or are words your friends?
- Are you a creative thinker, or are spreadsheets your specialty?
- Do you need a lot of feedback and praise? Do you need to see the results of your labors?
- Can you be a self-starter, take a rough idea and run with it?

Think about all these things until a clear picture forms in your mind of your absolute ideal job. Then write a description of that job here:

_____

_____

_____

_____

_____

_____

_____

_____

_____
_____
_____
_____
_____
_____
_____
_____
_____
_____
_____
_____
_____
_____
_____
_____
_____
_____

desk. I like problem solving, and I work best when I have clear incentives to perform well. Money motivates me, as I have a lot of student loans to pay off. Secretly I've always been attracted to high-end products and fantasized being able to afford the finer things in life. I'm comfortable around successful people, maybe because I hope some of their success will rub off on me.

The task now is to see the larger patterns, to extrapolate from your dream job some more realistic options. With her mentor, Sharisha was able to identify these potential job options based on her dream job description:

• hospitality or special events at a luxury resort
• Commissioned sales at a designer boutique
• Guest relations on a cruise ship
• Traveling rep for high-end cosmetics company, doing makeovers in department stores

So where did Sharisha end up? Selling luxury cars—Jaguars—in a major California city, which got her out and about on test drives and mingling with the kind of clientele she enjoyed. It turned out that she has a real gift for that sort of selling

Here's where it gets real

In a moment, you're going to take another look at what you wrote, looking for clues. For example, here's what Sharisha wrote in her workbook:

In my dream job I'm able to go outdoors part of the time. I like being around a lot of people, and I don't mind dealing with the public. There's no need for a special office; I'd rather be moving around in a larger space, not tied to a

situation, and she's made more money than she ever imagined possible. (In a job she never saw herself doing!)

An ad hinting at the high income potential caught her eye. However, she didn't just waltz into the dealership and land the job. She researched what kinds of sales experience she would need and made a point to get some. She studied the luxury car business and learned how to talk knowledgably about engine performance. She visited lots of dealers and took test drives in order to observe—and quiz—people already doing the job she wanted. Six months later, another sales position opened up, and Sharisha confidently swooped in and got it.

Now I know some of you are thinking: *Gee, that doesn't sound like a lifelong career.* True, Sharisha may one day tire of selling fast cars. But guess what? **Being good with the public and selling high-ticket items are VERY portable skills that she can take to all sorts of other venues.** In fact, with those abilities and a great track record, she can live anywhere in the country she wants to. Also, in a larger company, sales people often move up to managerial positions, should that ever become appealing to her.

Bridge Builder: So let's reexamine your dream job description. Involve your Champion Mentor in this process, as she'll have a broader picture of the company you work for, as well as a larger vision of what you might aspire toward. If your company has one, study your organizational chart. (See sample on Page 198.)

Make a list of possible jobs that would include at least several of the qualities you wrote about—both ones you feel ready for now and others to grow toward, but especially ones that might become available within your current organization. Ask your mentor for input if you're stumped or need help understanding your company's organizational chart.

—————————————————
—————————————————
—————————————————
—————————————————
—————————————————
—————————————————
—————————————————
—————————————————
—————————————————
—————————————————

Now rank them from 1-10 according to your current enthusiasm for each one.

Now ask yourself: Which job makes your pulse increase (in a good way)? Which one energizes you just thinking about it? Which one makes you smile even as you contemplate doing it? **That's the one to go after first.** If that job (or something similar) already exists where you work now, then you're all set. If it doesn't exist (or if you don't *know* if it exists) read on.

WORSHEET: Skill Development

GOAL: Identify your passions, interests, skills OUTSIDE of work that might come into play in your next job. In the first column, list things you've already done that could apply as well as any new activities you might like to explore to expand your experience.

Then in the second column, note portable skills you learned (or might learn) from each of these activities that you can apply to your career advancement. For example, your list might include:

• Tutor Spanish speaking teens after school (training and second language skills)

• Take art classes at the local museum on Saturdays (design aptitude, ready for further on-the-job training in new software)

• Spend your free time treasure hunting at garage sales, then you turn the items into something better and sell them for a profit on ebay (resourcefulness, accounting skills)

ACTIVITY

_____

_____

_____

_____

_____

_____

_____

_____

_____

_____

_____

_____

_____

_____

_____

_____

_____

SKILL LEARNED

_____

_____

_____

_____

_____

_____

_____

_____

_____

_____

_____

_____

_____

_____

_____

_____

_____

From the previous list, note the talents and skills you most want to put to work in your next position and brainstorm with your mentors about ways to use them.

_____

_____

_____

_____

_____

_____

_____

_____

_____

_____

_____

_____

_____

_____

_____

_____

_____

_____

_____

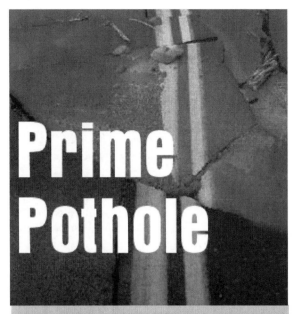

Prime Pothole: I realize some of you don't easily see a different vision for your future, and perhaps you feel stuck where you now work, afraid to leave all the benefits you've accrued. It may be that there just isn't a better job for you where you now work. Partly it may be a case of a known hell seeming preferable to an unknown heaven. **If you're already unhappy where you are now, it can be really difficult to turn that around.** It can be done, but it takes enormous energy and a willing manager to help make it happen. For you, I would suggest doing as much of the process in this guidebook as you can in order to prepare for a change. Then quietly and discreetly search for a new position while retaining your current job. Also, be careful to pick one that doesn't seem like too radical a departure from what you're doing now, as that will reduce the stress of adjusting to a new job.

WORKSHEET: What Other Destinations Could I Explore?

GOAL: If you've determined you need to look outside your current place of employment (or if you're unemployed) you need to brainstorm what sort of companies appeal to you that might also have the kind of jobs you've identified as being a good fit for you. On this list, you don't have to be too specific (unless you want to). For example, just listing a category such as department store or health food company is enough for this first phase.

CHAPTER SIX
Road Work Ahead

Identifying key gaps in your career path

Now you've arrived at the heart of this process: learning to review your employment history and your accumulated skills to compare them to the jobs you want to go after. As you examine the descriptions for the jobs you want, you may start to see things that are missing from your on-the-job experiences, from your education or both. **These holes in your resume are likely to keep you from attaining the promotion or the new job you seek.** Understanding what these gaps are is the key to advancement, because if you don't know what's wrong, you're not likely to fix it. Not to worry, we'll cover repairs in the next chapter.

> ## My term for this process is **career gap analysis.**

Other people may use different terms for filling in the gaps, such as punching all your

tickets, doing your time, etc.

Whatever you call them, these gaps can be as dangerous as a road washed out from a flood—these gaps can keep you stuck in low-paying, dead-end jobs. Over the course

of my own career in management, I began to see that people didn't get jobs because they had these gaps. Over time, for those who I mentored, it was filling in those gaps that shifted them into winning the jobs they went after.

You may be having a light bulb

moment right now if you've ever wondered why you got passed over for promotion, even though you know you do a great job and always receive great feedback. The critical point to understand is**: no matter how well you're currently performing, if you can't demonstrate the additional skills and/or experience that will be required of you at the NEXT level, you're not likely to get there.** I know it doesn't seem fair, but that's how many large organizations function. Managers know this. Executives know this. And they tend to handpick employees to share this knowledge with, to make sure they're the ones who *do* get the requisite assignments to beef up their resumes. But I promise you, it's definitely possible to detour around those roadblocks. Your Number One Guide through this will be your mentor. (If you're hopping around in the book, be sure to read the section on mentors, beginning on Page 33.)

There's another important point I want to make: **these gaps ONLY show up when you compare your resume to a new**

position that stretches you, that expands your abilities, that causes you to grow and advance in your career.

These gaps are not something bad, they don't signify anything about your performance or choices or anything like that. In fact, if you're content to stay on a very narrow career track with slow upward movement, then this whole process may not be relevant to you. However, if you do want to challenge yourself to see just how far you can go, to test more possibilities, then this is the route to take.

For now, let's focus on determining what your own gaps are. This is precisely the secret sauce that can flavor the rest of your career and your life, so even if it doesn't seem exciting yet, trust me—this really is the game changer. If you already have an intuitive hunch what some of your gaps might be, go ahead and jot them down here.

_____

_____

_____

_____

_____

_____

_____

_____

_____

_____

_____

Some mountains can't be climbed—at least not via the same old path

Meet Grace, a frustrated woman in her early 30s with an English degree from a prestigious college. At first, she assumed her degree would open many doors for her, and she'd quickly sail into some glamorous writing job. Right out of school she took an entry-level position as an administrative assistant in an advertising agency. So far so good. Yet ten years later she'd only advanced to be an assistant to one of the executives. Every time a copywriting job opened up at her agency, she applied for it— and every time she was passed over. Grace was beginning to wonder if there was a conspiracy against her, after all, she knew she was a good writer—why didn't anyone give her a chance to prove it?

Maybe you can spot the error in her thinking. Writing jobs rarely go to people who haven't *already* proven they're good writers. The only kind of writing Grace had done on the job were memos and budget reports, not exactly scintillating ad copy.

Moving Beyond Barriers

I know this can seem like a Catch 22: how could Grace get the needed experience if no one would give her a chance to try? In this situation the answer requires more creative thinking. These are some of the ways Grace might gain experience and those all-important writing samples:

- Find other opportunities to write, perhaps a regular newsletter for a group she belongs to

- Do a column in a neighborhood paper

- Start her own blog on a suitable topic— observations on trends in pop culture, a travel guide to her city or even local restaurant reviews

- If that's too ambitious, she can write guest posts on other people's blogs

- Join her local professional advertising association and volunteer to work on their projects

- Ask a local non-profit group if they need help with marketing or promotional copy— they're often open to offers of free help

- Pick bad examples of local advertising and rewrite them

She might even try her hand at writing a campaign for one of the agency clients

All these activities could result in writing samples for her passport (Page 62) **which is exactly the kind of proof of ambition that's needed to land a copywriting job.** After adopting this approach, within a year Grace was happily settled into a writing job, an office with a window and a bigger dream. **But it all started with finally understanding she had a gap in her experience.**

If this story resonates with you, do you have a similar gap between the kind of work you've been doing and the sort of work you want to do? If so, note it here:

_____

_____

_____

_____

_____

_____

_____

_____

_____

_____

Been there, filled my gaps

Here's what Jennifer, a former mentee of mine, has to say about the process.

"Gap analysis is a powerful career development tool for three key reasons:

1. Assembling your career documentation (your passport) gives you incredible insight into where you've been throughout your career, what you've learned and what your capabilities are. To see that all mapped out is incredibly empowering.

2. The Job Requirements Analysis (See worksheet, Page 112) challenges you to chart your path, down to the exact skills, visibility and learning experiences you need to advance in your organization. Don't skip this!

3. Gap analysis is impressive. That sounds superficial, but it opens doors for you. I've had three of my own managers who have been blown away by my work experience documentation. Plus two potential managers with whom I interviewed decided to spend time with me during and after the interview to quiz me about the gap analysis process."

Seeing an unlimited horizon

Another former mentee, Carolyn, is also enthusiastic about the process. "I'm an excellent example of the ease and success of using the gap analysis tool for evaluating career objectives, opportunities and ultimately exceeding my previous expectations. The gap analysis tool is designed to encourage you to look beyond obvious career progression paths and explore positions that leverage your skill sets and experience. The tool also reveals how you might pursue your own passion."

That's a great point she makes about obvious paths. **Don't be afraid to veer off the trail you've been on—there's nothing wrong with being a trailblazer.**

Carolyn continues: "When I first used the gap analysis process, I was in an executive development program and had a successful and productive career in Quality Assurance. It hadn't occurred to me or my leadership team to consider anything else for me. The process requires you to map your career journey and understand what motivates and excites you personally and professionally. The process of evaluating potential opportunities and meeting with current job holders and their leadership facilitate educated decision making." Note how she references what excites you. That's why I had you do the work in the last chapter of dreaming beyond your known world.

She concludes: "The initiative you take will be recognized and appreciated at every step. As a result of Carol's mentoring and her structured approach to career development, I was promoted into a senior leadership position in the Material Management organization. I've also been able to develop and practice my passion for continuous improvement. **As I continue to grow and revise my development plan, I truly understand that the future holds unlimited possibilities.**"

I couldn't have said it better myself—which is why I let her say it!

Are you suddenly feeling inspired to explore new options, side roads on your career journey that might be more fun or fulfilling? Just earning more money, a new job title or a bigger office rarely satisfies on a deeper level. **The more you can connect your career goals to your values and passions, the more authentic joy you'll find in your job.** If there are new options you might want to consider, list them here:

_____

_____

_____

_____

_____

_____

_____
_____
_____
_____
_____
_____
_____
_____

What if you want to change everything?

Sometimes embarking on this journey of self-examination leads to a desire to turn your life upside down, to overhaul your career goals and really go after your true dreams. That, of course, can be wildly intimidating. I want you to hear Becky's story, as she's someone who did exactly that and succeeded in a difficult type of transition.

Becky was already in the middle of her career, comfortable in a good job she'd held for twenty years with the state of Washington. She'd been a planner, grant writer and manager with a variety of good skills, but with zero experience outside the public sector.

"I had a skill set that met the requirements of my new private sector employer, but I had to learn their business. It was scary to sever a twenty-year relationship and the associated public servant mentality, but I was also excited to join a private, Fortune 500 company."

Becky soon identified two

significant differences between public and private employment, which she details here:

1. Your career is determined by what you're willing to put into it. Ask yourself these questions:

- Are you willing to learn—not just during your working hours, but on your own time?

- Are you open to critical advice? It's never easy to hear your weaknesses.

- Are you willing to change what needs improvement? This is not easy or natural—people hate change.

- Are you willing to do less desirable jobs while working toward your ultimate position?

2. You cannot advance on your own. You need mentors, you have to let your management know your goals, you have to build professional relationships and you have to perform well.

"For me, the gap analysis was easy to understand—I didn't have the technical knowledge that years of work at my new company would have naturally built, and I

hadn't grown up professionally in the company culture. I was fortunate to be accepted into an executive development program which required me to seek out mentors, write and present a career development plan to upper management."

For Becky, her biggest challenge was plunking herself into unknown territory and the insecurities that rose as a result.

"I always believed you had to have the knowledge base before you could perform and provide value. What I've learned is that knowledge gives you the power and confidence to negotiate an end result, but your portable skills can provide the initial leverage to enter a new business and offer merit. But you must be ready to learn, learn and learn!"

Becky makes a great point there, that change can be daunting, especially to someone already well along in her career. She had to be willing to start over in many ways and learn a whole new business and a whole new way of working. **If you're contemplating such a major career change, please be sure you have the attitude and energy for the long haul.** It may seem inviting to hop into an exciting new field, but in order to excel anywhere plenty of hard work is required. This is never more important than during challenging times, when businesses of all stripes are evaluating their personnel for the true value they contribute.

U-Turn Checklist

Circle all that apply to you:

• I have plenty of free time to research and study for my new job on my own.

• I'm a good student and love learning new things.

• I'm a self-starter who's good at motivating myself to do what's needed to reach my goals.

• I'm able to stay focused on the task at hand; I'm not easily distracted.

• I have a strong desire to try something totally new.

• I'm not hobbled by fear in new situations or meeting and working with new people.

• Change actually appeals to me; I get bored in the same old situations.

• I take constructive criticism well, in fact I welcome it, because it helps me grow.

• I actively apply new ideas to improve myself and my interpersonal skills.

• I enjoy challenges, they fire me up and stimulate my creativity.

• I accept that I may have to take a demotion, less pay and less status in order to start over in a new field.

• I'm willing to do whatever tasks I'm assigned in order to learn my new business.

• I'm naturally curious and am comfortable asking others for input, feedback and information. I never met a fact I couldn't save for a rainy day.

- I recognize that this U-turn may not work out for me, that I may have regrets, and I accept this risk.

Now add up how many you circled. Does it look like you have what it could take to turn your life inside out? Now look at the items you did NOT circle. What do those tell you about your readiness? I'm not saying you have to have all these qualities to successfully make a big career leap, but the more you can claim, the better. I urge you to review this list with your mentors if you're seriously contemplating this sort of move. **This would also be a great time to talk to your Faultfinder Mentor** (Page 43). Ask him what he thinks about this sort of leap. He's sure to think of potholes that you haven't.

How to escape a dead end

Not all changes need to be as severe as Becky's. I'd like to tell you story about a finance manager who came to work for me.

Arlene transferred from Sunnyvale, California and her background was mostly in finance, but it became obvious that she had lots of other skills, too. She was a very good analyst, she was excellent at determining what needed to be done to solve problems, she was highly motivated and she was a fast learner. **That told me Arlene had the potential to move up to the next level of leadership**, but unfortunately in our company there wasn't a higher level of leadership in her field.

So here I am with a talented finance person, but in order for her to progress to a higher level manager in our organization, she would actually have to change—or at least expand—the whole focus of her career. (Though certainly an understanding of finance can be useful in many departments.) I really felt Arlene had the ability to stretch and learn a lot more, so we agreed that I would give her assignments outside her regular duties: coordinating inputs to customer requests, doing "what if" exercises and sitting in for several of the other senior managers. This gave her experience in different departments as well as visibility with my peers and bosses.

I continued to have Arlene do special assignments that rounded out her skill sets, and even more importantly, I gave her projects where she'd be able to interface with my boss and my peers—people likely to be on selection panels for positions she might go after. I asked Arlene to give presentations at customer meetings, which revealed her talent in that area. She demonstrated good

communication and interpersonal skills working on teams with people from all over the country. As time went on, she continued to grow and learn more and more about the operation. When a senior manager position in scheduling opened up, Arlene applied for the job and won.

I'm certain that if she hadn't gone through that development process (and documented it all) with only her experience as finance manager she would not have won the position. Don't forget that maintaining good documentation of your career throughout this journey really helps make you more competitive, especially if other people aren't doing the same level of preparation. **Just because you progress to middle management, doesn't mean you should stop documenting your achievements—this is a lifelong activity.**

So what about you—**do you think you're stalled at a career dead end?** If so, it can help to sort it out by delineating it

more clearly. Take some time to write out the reasons you think you're in this situation. They might include: no discernible job to aspire to, no support for your

advancement, no passion for the kind of work at the next level of advancement, etc. Note your reasons here:

_____

_____

_____

_____

_____

_____

_____

_____

_____

_____

_____

_____

_____

Did Arlene's story resonate with you? Can you think of similar ways you might adjust your thinking in order to move off of your dead end street? they might include: retraining, finishing a degree, moving to a different branch, trying out assignments in other departments. Note your ideas here:

_____
_____
_____
_____
_____
_____
_____
_____
_____
_____
_____
_____
_____
_____
_____
_____

Compass Point

Lose your wobbly ladders. As you begin to identify your gaps, also examine the *shape* of your career. If you were to graph your job experience through an

organizational chart, what would it look like? A fairly straight upward line? One that zigs and zags with ups and downs? Or one that moves laterally as well as vertically?

If you look at the difference between a pyramid and a ladder it's easy to see a pyramid is much more structurally sound and incapable of wobbling. All too frequently when people talk about making progress in their careers they talk about climbing the ladder. Many people only look at the person above them and the one beyond to determine where they're aiming.

> The truth is, building a career on a pyramid is always going to be more stable and puts you in a position of strength rather than weakness.

In larger organizations, it also positions you to compete for multiple jobs, so your progression can be through numerous paths rather than just one, as we just saw with Arlene.

Whenever you work on your development plan with your manager and your mentor, think about building your career in the form of a pyramid. Look not only at positions above you, but also at positions horizontal to you that might broaden your background and experience. If you design a development plan in this manner, you'll find many more opportunities to grow in your career.

An example of moving horizontally would be to keep a similar job title and responsibilities but in a different department, where you can learn new information about how your company functions. This might mean moving from manufacturing to quality assurance, from engineering to product assurance, engineering to safety, manufacturing to production control or just about any other combination you can think of. By moving horizontally, the increase in your overall knowledge of the organization will make you a better leader and decision maker.

How would you draw the shape of your career so far?

Over my long career I saw endless variations on gap blindness:

- Jenna finally accepted a reality check—she thought she WAS qualified for jobs she went after and couldn't understand why she never got them. She kept confusing current competency with the requirements of the *next* job.
- Bert could only see the corporate ladder; his eyes were fixated on getting annual raises and he thought the only route to that prize was up. Once he embraced his gaps, he became inspired with an equal zeal to fill them, and he quickly began building bridges over them.
- Lisa truthfully didn't know what she wanted. Her career goals were unfocused, unrealistic and therefore unachievable, even though she considered herself to be ambitious. ("I'd love to run the company by the time I'm 30.") Once she got focused on attainable goals by means of a logical progression of advancements, she was on her way to achieving them. **She may well run the company someday—but not without a plan to get there.**

WORKSHEET: The Roads Not Taken

Think back to any promotions or jobs you went after but lost, and list them in the first column; in the second column list reason(s) why you know (or think) you didn't get the job. Then in the third column note if you now feel the outcome was fair—in other words, was there a legitimate gap in your resume that affected the hiring outcome?

_____   _____   _____

_____   _____   _____

_____   _____   _____

_____   _____   _____

_____   _____   _____

_____   _____   _____

_____   _____   _____

_____   _____   _____

_____   _____   _____

_____   _____   _____

_____   _____   _____

_____   _____   _____

_____   _____   _____

_____   _____   _____

_____   _____   _____

_____   _____   _____

_____   _____   _____

_____   _____   _____

_____   _____   _____

Now see if any of those gaps still seem important today as you consider new positions to seek. Circle any that deserve more study and attention.

WORKSHEET: Job Requirements

GOAL: Fully describe each position you are interested in pursuing. On the following pages, list the requirements for the position. Look at skills, abilities, experience and educational requirements.

Those can be determined through talking to your manager, mentor and Human Resources representative.

Let's get moving

Gather the worksheets you filled out in the last chapter (Page 96-98) as well as your Career Passport (Page 62), Mapping My Work History (Page 76) and notes from this chapter. **Make plenty of room and time to spread this all out and go on an expedition to secure your future.**

Then fill out the following worksheet(s) regarding those jobs you're most interested in that you identified on Page 95.

In some cases interviewing the person currently holding the job (or a similar one) can be helpful.

For each requirement determine if you meet it. Does this position use your strengths? Do your weaknesses hurt your ability to compete for the job? **Circle each requirement that is not met or is weak and add it to your Gap List on Page 120.**

JOB TITLE: _____

Department: _____   **Supervisor:** _____

Required qualities and/or skills:

_____

_____

_____

_____

Required education:

_____

_____

_____

_____

Work experience or product knowledge needed:

_____

_____

_____

_____

_____

_____

Personal qualities or traits needed for this job:

_____

_____

_____

_____

_____

_____

JOB TITLE:_____

Department: _____   **Supervisor:**_____

Required qualities and/or skills:

_____

_____

_____

_____

Required education:

_____

_____

_____

_____

Work experience or product knowledge needed:

_____

_____

_____

_____

_____

_____

_____

Personal qualities or traits needed for this job:

_____

_____

_____

_____

_____

_____

JOB TITLE: _____

Department: _____   **Supervisor:** _____

Required qualities and/or skills:

_____

_____

_____

_____

Required education:

_____

_____

_____

_____

Work experience or product knowledge needed:

_____

_____

_____

_____

_____

_____

_____

Personal qualities or traits needed for this job:

_____

_____

_____

_____

_____

_____

_____

Sometimes your journey is also a competition

Many of us shy away from confrontations, contests and any kind of competition. Women often prefer compromise, cooperation and making nice. That's fine, but if you're serious about going after higher and higher level positions, you must accept the fact that there will probably be other people going after the same jobs. Sometime LOTS of other people. There's no getting around it, at various points in your career journey you're going to face competition. Once you accept that reality, why not win? No one likes to lose. **And the beauty of this process is, you'll have many advantages over your competition.**

But first it can help to understand your competitors. Now this part will likely seem really foreign to most readers. That's because we don't often need to think like this in business. And it's not meant to be a sneaky or underhanded endeavor—think of it as a research project. Of course you can't expect to know who's going to apply for a position from outside your company, so **this just pertains to other people within your organization who may be seeking the same job you are.**

This is where your mentors and network of colleagues can be invaluable. Ask them to check around and find out who else might be in the running for any of the positions on your list. Then you'll want to learn more about their background and readiness for those jobs. As you gather this information, add it to the following worksheet. Of course, if you work at a rather small company with no one to compete with, then none of this will be necessary, and you can hop ahead to the next worksheet.

WORKSHEET: Other Travelers I May Meet

GOAL: evaluate your competition as a way of improving your own preparedness.
Who is your competition? Identify names of people who you expect to be your competition. How would you rank for each requirement against each competitor? Identify where you score lower than the competition or where you are missing useful experience. Add those to your Gap list.

COMPETITOR	JOB REQUIREMENT	THEIR RANK	MY RANK
_____	_____	_____	_____
_____	_____	_____	_____
_____	_____	_____	_____
_____	_____	_____	_____
_____	_____	_____	_____
_____	_____	_____	_____
_____	_____	_____	_____
_____	_____	_____	_____
_____	_____	_____	_____
_____	_____	_____	_____
_____	_____	_____	_____
_____	_____	_____	_____
_____	_____	_____	_____
_____	_____	_____	_____
_____	_____	_____	_____
_____	_____	_____	_____
_____	_____	_____	_____
_____	_____	_____	_____
_____	_____	_____	_____
_____	_____	_____	_____

Get to know your gatekeepers

In larger corporations, hiring or promotion decisions are often made by committee or a selection panel. I've mentioned them before, as well as the importance of making yourself known to higher-ups who may well sit on one of your panels one day. Getting to know those people can make all the difference in your getting the job you want. **Again, this is the kind of information that is best acquired by your mentors.**

WORKSHEET: Selection Panel Analysis

GOAL: Determine what steps you need to take to optimize your chances.

Who will be on the panel selecting this position? Highlight on the organization chart who will be responsible for filling each position of interest. Some may do interviews or in other cases their decisions may be based on what they already know about you. Sometimes it will all come down to your resume and any additional documentation you provide. Ask yourself if each panel member knows you and is familiar with your talents and experience. If not add that person's name to your Gap List.

POSITION	PANELIST	DO THEY KNOW ME?

POSITION	PANELIST	DO THEY KNOW ME?

Gap List: Where There's Space For Improvement

List all the gaps you've identified from doing the worksheets in this chapter.

Work Experience Gaps

_____

_____

_____

_____

Job Requirements Gaps

_____

_____

_____

_____

Competition Gaps

_____

_____

_____

_____

Selection Panel Visibility Gaps

_____

_____

_____

_____

By now you should have a clear idea of what's missing in your training and experience. Even if it's a long list, don't despair. **I want to reiterate here: gaps are not bad or indicative of failures on your part. They simply reveal what else you need to know in order to progress in your career journey.**

Some of these potholes can be fixed more easily than you'd think. We'll put on our hard hats in the next chapter. **Then you'll be fully prepared to attain any fabulous new job you want to go after.** So what are you waiting for? Let's keep going!

CHAPTER SEVEN
Filling In Your Gaps

Developing a plan for creating your best career

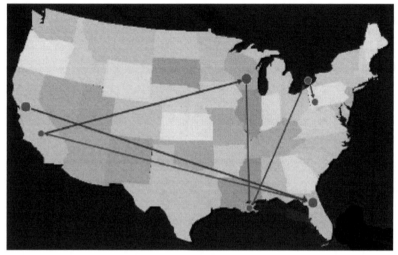

Whether your career map has a few potholes or needs major construction, it will be much easier to accomplish with a solid, well thought out plan. So that's what we're going to focus on in this chapter. This might be a fairly simple thing that will only take a few months, or it could entail years of classes if you suddenly realized you really do want that advanced degree.

> **Try not to focus on the time element—this is a long-term strategy to lay a secure foundation for the rest of your working life.**

Take out your list of all the gaps you've identified from doing the worksheets in this book (Page 120). They could include gaps from these worksheets:

· **Job Requirements Gaps**
· **Work Experience Gaps**
· **Competition Gaps**
· **Selection Panel Visibility Gaps**

Your first activity is to meet with your mentors, study your Gap List and determine how many of your goals can be achieved within your current work environment and how many will need effort outside of your workplace. (For example, whether you can volunteer for extra assignments to broaden your experience, or whether you just need to take night classes in accounting.)

FIXING JOB REQUIREMENT GAPS: Avoiding school daze

Let's start with the known requirements of positions you're interested in going after. **If there are obvious gaps in your formal education or skill training, then now is the time to research your options and set a plan in motion.** Since this could take significant time, get this aspect of your plan in action at the outset. Knowing you're making progress in that arena will motivate you in other areas, too. As you begin to apply what you're learning to your current job, don't be surprised if your boss notices, which in turn could lead to more responsibility and other positive changes that are on your To Do List.

If you have a glaring education gap,

I'm sure you're feeling overwhelmed. When are you supposed to fit that into your busy life? In our 24/7 world that never seems to sleep, it can seem like there's rarely any real free time. Which is why one of the first things you could do is **record how you spend ALL your time for one week**. It may sound like a silly exercise, but I promise you, it can yield hidden riches of opportunities. For example, taking a commuter train to work instead of your car might give you five extra hours a week to study. (And you might arrive at work less stressed in the bargain!)

    Undoubtedly there will be personal / family / social activities that need your attention on weekends. We all have to do laundry sometime. **That's why I place emphasis on finding as much time as you can during your work week.** For one thing, it's easier to focus on educational goals when your mind is already occupied with your current job. For another thing, you do need some time to recharge each week,

which is why it's usually a bad idea to put off your studying until the weekend. (Especially if you were the kid who started your book reports at 9 p.m. on Sunday nights when they were due Monday morning.)

 **NOTE:** Even if you don't need more training, you'll still need to set aside time for related activities such as: working on your passport, researching other job options, reading trade publications in your field, and so on. This worksheet will help you find the time.

WORKSHEET: Where Does All My Time Go?
WORK DAYS
- What time do you get up?
- What time do you leave for work?
- Can you imagine getting up earlier?

How much time could be gained **before work** to carve out some study time?

_____

_____

_____

_____

_____

_____

- What's your method of **commuting**—is there time there that could be better used? If so, how much?

_____

_____

_____

_____

_____

_____

• Circle this if a different method of **commuting** would provide some free time.

• What errands do you do **before work**? Could someone else do them? How much time would that free up for you?

_____

_____

_____

_____

_____

_____

_____

_____

_____

_____

_____

• How much time are you allotted for **lunch**? What options are there to get away to a quiet place to study for 20 or 30 minutes? (Earbuds in an MP3 player can solve a lot of noise problems.)

_____

_____

_____

_____

_____

_____

• What errands and activities do you typically do **on the way home**? Could some or all of those be reassigned in order to reach some short-term goals? Even just clearing your schedule for the first month of your return to school can be enough to get you going. How much time could you gain here?

_____

_____

_____

_____

_____

_____

_____

_____

_____

_____

_____

_____

• Do you do all the **meal** planning, shopping and cooking? That's a big hunk of time every week. Who could take over for awhile? Or how about eating out on class nights? You can always review class reading and notes during your meal. Note time gained from changes here:

_____

_____

_____

_____

_____

• If you're more of a night person, then **evenings** may be where you can grab some quality time for your classes. How much time each weeknight could you realistically devote to study?

_____

_____

_____

• **Total up all the potential extra time you've identified:**_____

WEEKENDS

• How much time do you need on average for household activities? Any recruits possible to help for awhile?

_____

_____

_____

_____

_____

_____

_____

_____

_____

_____

_____

• How much time for **socializing**? If it's usually a lot, how about cutting back just for awhile?

_____

_____

_____

_____

_____

• How much true **down time** do you need to refuel yourself?

_____

_____

_____

• Is there realistically any time left over on a typical weekend to use for **school** work or other career projects? If so, how much? _____

• **Add up all the potential extra time from your weekends:**_____

Grand Total of extra time you've identified for a typical week: _____

Now before you commit to an ambitious schedule of night school, see if the class requirements match your available a time. (And to be reasonable, you can probably halve that Grand Total Time Found number, unless you were conservative in your assessment.) Life happens. Your schnauzer suddenly needs a trip to the vet. Johnny needs new shoes. Your car needs to go in for repairs. Best laid plans and all that.

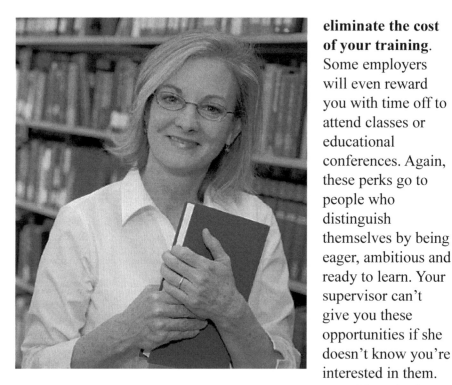

> **But even after you cut that fantasy time number in half, I believe most people can round up an extra ten hours or more most weeks.**

If your life really is crammed already, then it may come down to sacrificing some precious sleep in order to meet your long-term goals. If that's your dilemma, then start slowly. Don't sign up for more than one class and pick the easiest one to begin with.

Your Human Resources Department and/or your manager should be informed about all kinds of options—just ask. In addition, **many companies provide education vouchers to offset or even eliminate the cost of your training**. Some employers will even reward you with time off to attend classes or educational conferences. Again, these perks go to people who distinguish themselves by being eager, ambitious and ready to learn. Your supervisor can't give you these opportunities if she doesn't know you're interested in them.

Also, don't overlook in-house training options. Many companies today have lots of training available, either online, on DVDs that you can take home, or classes on site or off. Be willing to take these classes on your own time if necessary.

An example from my own career was when I was transferred to a new group in manufacturing. The first thing I did was view all the shop training videos. (Many, many hours of these videos.)

Was it the most fun way to spend my weekends? No. Did it make all the difference in how quickly I adapted to my new job? Absolutely!

The videos helped me with terms and acronyms, and that in turn helped me connect with my team more quickly and understand the challenges of each aspect of my department.

Developing your career outside the workplace

Advancement can happen anywhere. Detours don't have to be bad things. If you don't have an HR department full of resources, don't despair. There are many other ways to grow and increase your talent outside your workplace. Many professional organizations, community service organizations, charities, societies, religious organizations and training organizations offer networking and educational opportunities. **Even brief workshops can do you a world of good—especially when you document what you learned, as we discussed on Page 61.**

Some opportunities may come to you when someone asks you to join a group. Others you'll need to seek out for yourself. Be open to taking on some of these challenges and opportunities. You can practice leadership, strategic planning, budgeting, organizational abilities and a variety of other skills away from your job.

★ Does your son's school need help publicizing a big fundraising event?

★ Can you help organize your church's canned food drive?

★ How about volunteering to be on your local library board and offering to do their monthly newsletter?

★ Could you join the Chamber of Commerce and become active on the membership committee?

★ Can you pursue a passion for blogging about recycling and turn that into demonstrated job skills?

I think you get the idea. Look into your local community colleges and training groups. Even if you have a bachelor's degree, there's always specialized training you can seek to add to your skills. **Think of education as a lifelong process rather than a one-time event.** And realize that everything you do outside of work has the potential to increase your job skills. There are likely to be numerous learning opportunities all around you—it may just take a shift in perspective. **If you can think of a few options to investigate, note them here.**

_____

_____

_____

_____

_____

_____

_____

_____

_____

_____

As you look at filling your gaps you can choose some of these options to get part or all of the experience you're missing, especially if your job site does not provide opportunities for developing the needed skills to fill in your gaps.

Be sure you consider ALL your education options. One of the best things about the internet is how easy it can be to take classes online. Whether it's a specialized one-time seminar or an ongoing class, you can often do it at *your* convenience and at your own pace. This is a HUGE advantage if it's been many years since you were in school, or if you have any learning challenges or old baggage about not being a good student and so on. **Online learning can reduce or eliminate most of the stress involved with school.** It can even offer you as much time as you need to complete your course work. (Just don't use it as an excuse to slow your pace to non-existent!)

You're not alone in the wilderness

Self-directed study can seem intimidating if you aren't used to it, but there are many helpful folks out there who've made it *their* career to help people just like you succeed at *your* career. Keep asking questions. Talk to librarians. Talk to career counselors at employment offices and agencies. Tell everyone you know what you need. Post questions in online forums and on Twitter and Facebook. Network. Schmooze. Be aggressive about getting what you need. This is your future at stake here!

Some options to examine:

✔ Specialized online skill training (in new software, for example).

✔ One-time online seminars (in sales techniques, for example). This type of course can often be downloaded and listened to whenever you like.

✔ Structured online classes—these may or may not have real-world time limits—be sure to determine that before you sign up. Also see if there will be live interactive features that you'll want to be available for.

✔ Home study courses with DVDs and other materials. These can come from your place of work or another source.

✔ Self-directed study using books, workbooks and other class materials. Spend some quality time perusing Amazon.com and you may be surprised to find there's book on how to do just about everything. In you're in doubt, print out the pages of description (along with user comments, which can be invaluable) and show them to your mentors for feedback.

✔ In-person instruction at a local community college.

✔ Night or weekend classes at a local university.

✔ Weekend workshops for hands-on learning of technical skills.

✔ One-on-one tutoring from a qualified expert in your field. This could be a great place to begin if you have issues with learning disabilities or if English is your second language.

Where there's a will there's a degree

Terri was an entry level new hire in our technical document center. I took a look at her resume and saw she came from the public sector and had some leadership experience from her years with the government. Terri came to me for mentoring, so we sat and talked—and her first gap was obvious: she didn't have a bachelor's degree, which was going to be needed for the direction she wanted to go.

So she signed her up for college, got tuition reimbursement and was able to go to the local university to finish her degree. Terri also started working on more gap

analysis with some of the other managers who volunteered to be her mentors. Thanks to them, she started taking on other assignments doing new duties while sitting in for managers who were away. She continued to develop and fill in the gaps in her experience, and within about two years she was promoted to manager. Continuing this process, Terri moved from position to position broadening her experience both horizontally and vertically.

Terri was one of those people who had given up on her dream of a college degree. As a racial minority woman in an overwhelmingly white male workforce, she'd been misperceiving what her true opportunities were. Plus she didn't see how she'd afford it or where she'd find the time. A funny thing happened once she learned we were picking up the tab—her enthusiasm level skyrocketed and she *made* the time to take advantage of this great opportunity.

You have two choices: you can be hesitant and not want to put in the work

or you can be enthusiastic, make the effort and gain all the benefits. It's always your choice.

Then there was Jerry. He was stuck at a low-level production job, and his attitude was heading farther and farther south each year. He made it clear to me that he'd always hated school and wasn't likely to go back anytime soon. Yet he needed to increase his income to support his growing family. Deeper questioning revealed that he'd never had good family or peer support for doing well in school. In fact, the good students in his high school were bullied and teased for their devotion to learning. Jerry never even graduated, something that was actually a source of shame for him, which he covered up with false bravado.

Once we got to the bottom of his problem and I assured him there was all kinds of help available to him, he started to come around. **The clincher was doing an income projection if he remained on the course he was on,** versus a different road that could lead to significant promotions and pay increases. Grasping a six-figure lifetime

earning difference was all it took to turn the tide.

The first class Jerry took was actually a one-time class in how to be a better student. That gave him the confidence to continue. Within five years Jerry got his GED, finished some community college classes, had doubled his income and surely quadrupled his self-esteem. All because a high school dropout found out it's never to late to drop back in.

What about you? Are there educational goals you've abandoned? If so, note them here.

_____

_____

_____

_____

_____

_____

_____

_____

_____

_____

_____

_____

_____

_____

WORSHEET: Education Plan To Expand Your Horizons

Skill needed:_____

Where or how you can learn it:_____

By what date do you want to learn this new skill:_____

How much will the training cost?_____

Is there company support for this training? Can they provide materials or funding?_____
_____

Do you need authorization for this program or class? If so, from whom?_____

Additional resources you can use (books, DVDs, etc.)_____
_____

Where you can get them:_____

Will you need help from groups or resources beyond your workplace? If so, what?_____
_____

Have you identified the extra time needed to devote to this plan?_____

Develop a plan to check in with your mentor on your progress:_____
_____

What documentation will prove you've mastered this skill?_____
_____

Have you added that to your passport?_____

Degree desired:_____

Work left to do to achieve this degree:_____
_____

Realistic time frame to reach this goal:_____

What schools are you considering?_____

Would online education be a better option?_____

What financial support do you need to achieve this?_____

Does your company offer any?_____

Outside funding sources scholarships, grants, business groups, etc.:_____
_____

What's the application process and schedule for the next term?_____

Check in with your Faultfinder Mentor: is this something you can expect to succeed at?_____

_____

If your goal is ambitious, break it down into manageable chunks one year at a time:_____

_____

_____

_____

_____

_____

_____

FIXING WORK EXPERIENCE GAPS: Be open to some side trips

The next category of gaps are holes in your work experience, and filling them can be an adventure if you're open to it. These gaps are really common, especially if you're in the early stages of your career, or if you've languished in one position too long. In addition to skill training and seeking more education, you can fill these gaps with hands-on experience. If you work at a large enough company and your mentors agree that it's possible, then **the easiest way to gain more experience is to get it right where you already work**. Everyone takes vacations, managers go away on business, people get sick, take family leave. During most of those situations, someone has to pick up the slack so the company can keep functioning. Rather than see those situations as burdensome times when you get overworked, take a new approach and view them as opportunities.

Humor me and consider these shifts:

Lucinda shares her story. Old attitude: "The office manager is going to be gone for three weeks, and I'll have to answer all her customer service emails, stay late on Friday to do the weekly inventory report, place bi-weekly orders for supplies, and handle all the walk-in customers on my own. I'll be lucky to get out of here before 6 o'clock most nights. All I'll get is a few extra hours of overtime—and griping from my husband because dinner will be late."

New attitude: "I've always coveted the job of office manager, so this is my chance to prove I can do it. Even if I don't get an opportunity to be promoted to the position here, demonstrating (and documenting!) that I can do it should help me get that sort of job in another company. I make sure to write really comprehensive replies to all the customer service emails and save copies of all exchanges. I ask plenty of questions *before* my manager leaves, so I understand exactly how to do her job well. In fact, I do such a good job with the inventory report that she turns it over to me permanently, which is a great thing to have for my career passport. I even manage to innovate some improvements to our inventory system, which saves the company money and earns me a great letter of commendation for my files—and even a nice bonus. My improved attitude at work is noticed, and somehow I manage to get more work done in less time and enjoy it more! Who knew?"

Rachel shares her story. Old attitude: "My boss is always going out of town to meetings, and though he thinks he handles everything from the road, there's always a lot of stuff that gets left for me to take care of while he's away. Stuff he never hears about, headaches he causes by being gone without leaving good notes and problems that need solving without him. It's a big fat pain, but I don't feel like I dare complain. I need this job and I have to stay in his good graces."

New attitude: "I decided to change how we handle his absences, because it dawned on me that perhaps he wasn't happy

with how it was going, either. I put myself in *his* place and tried to imagine his stress, worrying about how things were going back at the office. So well before his next trip, I scheduled some quality time to review our procedures. I'd already written a memo outlining my suggested changes to our routine. I gently let him know how disruptive his trips really were, and what I'd been doing to keep things afloat. I realized that keeping him in the dark about all that wasn't doing either of us a favor. In fact, he *was* glad to learn the truth of the situation, as he'd been wondering how things managed to go on without him so much of the time. Once he realized how efficient I was, he delegated a lot more of his responsibilities to me (along with a promotion to executive assistant and a resulting pay raise). Now I have the authority to handle things more professionally when he's gone, and he can concentrate on his sales calls without worrying about office matters. It's a win/win for us both. I ended up doing the same things—except that now I get credit for them AND paid for them, too!"

WORKSHEET: A Fork In Your Road

- Can you now see how you might have taken a different attitude had you known what a boon it could be to your career development?

_____

_____

_____

_____

_____

_____

- Are you aware of upcoming opportunities to sit-in for someone?

_____

_____

_____

_____

_____

_____

_____

- Can you think of situations when you felt overworked because of filling in for someone?

_____

_____

_____

_____

- If not, who would you *like* to fill in for? Who would you ask about that?

_____

_____

_____

_____

- What aspects of their job would you like to learn how to do?

_____

_____

_____

_____

_____

_____

_____

_____

- What skills could you learn or improve while filling in for them?

_____

_____

_____

_____

_____

_____

_____

- Ask your mentors to help set this up for you.

_____

_____

_____

- How will you document your time doing this fill-in assignment?

_____

_____

_____

_____

_____

_____

_____

_____

- What do you need to do to prepare for that *in advance*? (Bring a video camera to work, learn how to take screenshots on your computer, master a video capture program like Camtasia that could document your new computer skill *as you do it*!)

_____

_____

_____

_____

_____

_____

_____

_____

You have to ask for more work—yes, you really do!

Beyond taking initiative when situations thrust you into new activities, **you must also find the courage to ask for and take on challenging assignments**. Always be prepared take on any assignment. Your eagerness to learn and work hard will find you becoming the "go to" person in your organization.

Sure, asking to do something you've never tried can be scary. After mentoring for 35 years and coaching over 1,000 mentees, the most common skill they needed was having courage and becoming comfortable with a dose of fear. If you don't feel a little fear, you are most likely not learning and growing. Learn to love the feeling of stretching yourself beyond your previous limits and comfort zones. The pride you feel in your success is a great reward.

Learning opportunities can come in different forms:

★ You can seek special assignments, like gathering data for the annual report.

★ You can cross train with a co-worker, so you can do each other's jobs.

★ You can sit in for a leader who's on vacation as a way of test-driving another position and preparing you for leadership.

★ You might even make up your own opportunities by suggesting new projects that would benefit your department, company or your larger community. Perhaps you volunteer to organize a company-wide drive to collect donations for tornado victims in your area. Or maybe you rally your team to help build a Habitat for Humanity house. **Demonstrating that level of leadership is sure to get noticed.**

Seek out challenging assignments beyond your area of expertise, look for opportunities to be valuable to your organization. Then don't be shy about accepting credit—and thanks—for your good work. **Pop quiz: and what else should you do? Yes—DOCUMENT it all!**

Corrine learned her lesson and made sure her husband was on hand to video and photograph her hard at work on the house building project she took on. Then she collected letters of thanks and kudos for her organizational skills that she had demonstrated by making sure her company fielded a full team of workers every weekend for three months. A photo of her with the new home's owner standing on the finished front porch was the perfect summation to her report. Ultimately, Corrine discovered she loved that sort of community involvement so much that she sought out—and won—a great job working for Habitat

process as well as the end result. No one else they interviewed could display that level of dedication, so giving Corrine the job was an easy decision.

Watch out for this road hazard

Once your supervisor realizes your sincere commitment to self-improvement, he may well start to offer you various options and incentives. This is great, because it shows you that management supports your initiative and efforts. **Just be sure that if you accept the opportunities, they seem like they could contribute to your career advancement by developing new skills and giving you a taste of other job options.** If not, your boss may be trying to get you to do whatever needs doing that no one else is willing to do. He may mistake your new enthusiasm for a willingness to do anything and load you up with all the grunt work that everyone else complains about doing. I want you to turn into an opportunity seeker, not a doormat.

What to ask for in your development assignments

Be sure to discuss this thoroughly with your manager and mentor. You can ask for a myriad of assignments:

Volunteer for difficult jobs, not just the easy, fun ones. Let your hand be the first one in the air when help is needed.

for Humanity. Within six months she went from an office job that bored her to a new position that got her out in the community, traveling around her state and making a tangible difference in the lives of deserving families. As she says, "The joy I feel each time the keys are handed over to the family is the best job perk I have. I sleep really well at night, knowing I can personally change the course of people's lives to this degree. It's a humbling responsibility."

As she later told me, it was being able to actually see the enthusiasm on Corrine's face in her photo essay that convinced the organization to hire her. Lots of people can feign excitement during a job interview, but seeing her hard at work, up to her knees in mud as she helped pour a foundation, demonstrated her genuine love of the

Ask to sit in for other employees who are gone or on their own special assignments, especially if it's something you're *not* good at. Just be sure to make it clear that you see this as a growth experience for yourself and that you won't be as proficient as the person you're filling in for—at least not on Day One.

Offer to train interns or new hires—you'll be surprised how much *you* learn when you have to explain things to someone else.

Take on the gigantic projects no one else wants to tackle, ones that would vividly demonstrate your exceptional organizational skills.

> **This is the shortest route I know to winning over your boss and achieving Hero Status.**

Merilee did just that and it changed her life. *Really.* Less than a year into her job, she knew she hadn't yet made a big impression on her boss, but she couldn't figure out how to do that. Nor had she found her best fit within the insurance agency where she worked. Then an opportunity arose. Her boss wanted to digitize ten years' worth customer information that had been archived on paper only. The dusty files were overflowing a space that could be better used. No one else even knew where to start, but Merilee just made it up as she went along. Her boss was so thrilled that she was

attempting it, that he left her alone and let her make all the decisions about how to do it. She set aside one day a week to do the job and asked not to be interrupted. The kind of information she uncovered was staggering. She found all kinds of customers who needed attention, and those she set aside to call herself. Many were older folks whose policies were outdated. When she invited them to come in for a policy review, most accepted. In many cases, she actually saved customers money on their premiums due to newer pricing plans and bundling.

After two months of steady work on the project, not only had Merilee hit the halfway mark, she'd updated dozens of policies, brought in more than a dozen new clients from referrals and made her boss look like a hero to many of his most loyal customers.

So what skills was Merilee's boss able to appreciate about her after this experience?

✔ She's a master organizer

✔ She can see the big picture and design procedures to accomplish large goals

✔ She's a self-starter who's not afraid to take initiative

✔ She's willing to be held accountable for her decisions

✔ She makes good choices

✔ She recognizes unmet customer needs

✔ She jumps in to fill them ASAP

✔ She has great interpersonal skills and managed to transform what was actually a failure on the part of the agency into an opportunity to provide better customer care

✔ She's not afraid of hard work and always shows up with enthusiasm and a can-do attitude

✔ She's not a complainer

✔ She saw the underlying benefit to her project—the enhanced protection of their older customers

Who wouldn't want someone like that working for them? This project showed Merilee that she wanted to focus her time on client care and her boss agreed. He relieved her of her less exciting chores and gave her carte blanche to provide the best service possible for their customers. He also instituted financial incentives and bonuses for her work, so within a year of completing that awful project that no one wanted to do, Merilee had more than doubled her income AND doubled her job satisfaction. **All because she wasn't afraid of some dust and some diligent work.**

Using your evaluations to strengthen your weaknesses

Most people receive periodic evaluations on their job performance. Instead of focusing on the negatives or criticisms as something bad, I'd like you to realize they're actually a gift. Typically, feedback on your weaknesses will come in two ways: from your regular performance evaluation or as the result of not getting selected for a position. **It's important to use this feedback as a treasure map to what you can improve.** Your goal should be to seek developmental assignments which can help strengthen your weaknesses. Most of the time when people offer criticism it really is meant to help you improve, but if you're the sensitive type, it's easy to take it the wrong way. The things others point out about you are often things you don't realize about yourself (or don't want to acknowledge). **It can be a true time saver and shortcut to the top to have your weaknesses pointed out to you so you can fix them.**

The most common flaws are weaknesses in: **communication skills** (verbal, written, and presentation) and/or **interpersonal skills**. Every employee should take responsibility for their own development. Upon getting feedback you need to make sure that your development plan includes assignments which can strengthen your weaknesses. That said, do ask your mentors for advice on how to improve specific items.

confident you *are* making improvements. At that point, you might use these before and after examples to gain additional writing assignments. Plus your supervisor ought to appreciate your initiative. As for presentation skills, they're so important they get their own section.

In the area of **communication**, you can increase your verbal skills by considering opportunities such as Toastmasters. Push yourself to speak up more in meetings and offer your ideas. **Don't be afraid to be visible and be heard.** You can improve your written skills by volunteering to write white papers, reports, intra-office newsletters, and so on. Pay attention to all the written communication that passes by you. When you see great examples, copy them to a folder for further study. When you see documents that strike you as being less than they might be, try rewriting them yourself and see if you can improve them. You don't need to show these to anyone until you're

Ride your fear to greater heights

While taking on greater responsibilities and widening your scope, you need to make sure you use any opportunity to present your work to your leadership. We all know public speaking is challenging and intimidating, but **I urge you to do everything you can to get over your fear of giving presentations**. I remember when I was 23 and promoted to manager, it was clear to me I was going to have to speak in front of groups. In high school I even took an F in one class because I was too afraid of speaking in front of the class. So I knew I needed to do something. I decided to take a college class in giving speeches.

After practicing at school, I remember my first formal presentation to my boss. I was standing on the stage explaining some new procedure, pointing to something on the screen when my two-foot long pointer went flying across the room. You can imagine my embarrassment! But everyone broke out in laughter, and I was able to collect myself and finish the presentation. From then on, I looked for more opportunities to get experience giving presentations.

Whether speaking to just your team or department or to a large public gathering, presentation skills are something that can catapult you to ever higher levels in your career. This is partly because the number one fear in adults is public speaking. **Instead of being a statistic and shying away from opportunity, why not be the one in your office who relishes these situations?**

After all, that's precisely how you get higher-ups to see you in action (and remember you when promotion decisions are made). How do you improve at presenting? Opportunities abound once you're open to seeing them.

★ Look into college courses on public speaking.

★ Develop visual presentation skills, too—learn how to use PowerPoint and other useful tools.

★ There are some excellent books for advanced PowerPoint users—don't settle for being merely adequate.

★ Try teaching classes or leading trainings yourself.

★ Join the national speakers organization, Toastmasters, which provides education as well as opportunities to practice.

★ Volunteer to speak to groups you belong to on something you're already passionate about, as that helps ease fear.

★ Practice in front of a mirror or in front of your spouse.

★ Offer to give speeches at volunteer activities. Head up committees, so you'll be the one delivering the reports when you're done.

Next, let's look at your **interpersonal** skills and how to improve them. So what's included in this category? Anything that happens when you interact with another person, including but not limited to:

• your ability to make others feel comfortable

• being generous with compliments when warranted

• expressing gratitude when appropriate

• your level of tact, especially in sticky situations

• your ability to read a room of people and know what's needed

• your skill with understanding emotional intelligence

• how you handle difficult co-workers

• your attitude and level of enthusiasm for your job and how it affects others

• how well you cooperate with others

• are you constantly finding—and pointing out—faults in others?

• how you mesh with a team on a big project

• your reaction if you're asked to lead a group

• how you behave around clients

• your comfort level around executives

• your ability to mediate between people with opposing views

• the level of respect you show to your supervisor

• how well you handle feedback, especially criticism

When trying to improve your **interpersonal** skills, you should be looking at: books, classes and getting feedback from your friends and family. You can also take jobs where you interface with different levels of employees, which is a great way to develop tact and nuance. Or you could seek positions where you can liaison with union employees, or with other groups of workers, such as engineers.

> # The objective is to practice your interpersonal skills in new and more challenging situations.

Simply chatting with your direct peer group every break or lunch hour won't expose you to other points of view, or ways of self-expression.

Erin found this area especially challenging, but it kept coming up during her reviews, so she finally decided to conquer it. She was often perceived as reluctant, aloof, uncooperative and just not a team player. Being totally honest with herself, she could see where this originated. Erin is actually painfully shy and distances herself from any situation where she might be put on the spot or become the center of attention. As she says, "I actually enjoy working with groups of people—as long as I know them well and am comfortable with them. It's being thrust into new situations with strangers that causes me to clam up. What other people see as coldness is just fear on my part."

Once Erin accepted that her career advancement depended on overcoming this trait, she took radical steps to do just that. She hired a personal coach who gave her books to read, DVDs to watch and

specific assignments to gradually overcome her shyness. Once Erin realized her shyness was really fear of criticism, a shift in how she viewed feedback made all the difference. "Now when I speak up at work, people look at me differently. Co-workers who I thought didn't like me, now want to have lunch with me—turns out they thought I was stuck up. At my last review, my boss went on and on about my new attitude, and he all but promised me a promotion as soon as a slot opens up. And here I thought I would be shy for the rest of my life!"

If you think you have some interpersonal issues (and really, who doesn't?) **a useful tool is to take the Myers-Briggs assessment** to find out what your personal characteristics are, such as preferring to present yourself as extroverted or introverted. It can also reveal how suited you are to the job you have now and the kind of jobs you're interested in going after. It's beyond the scope of this book to delve into all the categories of results from this test, but it can be a really useful way to learn more about how you operate in a work environment.

Another excellent test is the Kolbe profile, which you can even take online. Kolbe measures to what degree you have an aptitude for detail work, as an innovator, as someone who is quick to begin new things or as someone who prefers to implement projects through to completion.

If you want to ensure you're in the right career, improve job satisfaction, enhance your competitive advantage by capitalizing on your strengths, please consider investing your time in these sorts of tests. They can be especially useful if you have vague feelings of unease in your career but don't know why, or if you know you're not in the right position but aren't sure what sort of job would be a better fit. **Knowledge is power, especially when it comes to finding the perfect fit in your career.** Talk to your HR department people, they may even be able to set up the testing for you.

Studies show that only 20 percent of employees enjoy jobs that really maximize their strengths. You undoubtedly contain a reservoir of ideas, experience and information that rarely gets tapped. **One of the keys to job satisfaction is knowing you have something of value to contribute and being acknowledged for it.** In a sense, that can be a different sort of gap—knowing there's untapped potential inside you just waiting to be harnessed.

That's how Sandy saw it, too. She works in publicity for a small publishing company and loves it. "I don't make as much money as I could working for a larger company," she explains, "but my boss is so spectacularly appreciative of everything I do for her, that I don't dream of changing jobs. I've never had a work experience like that—and I've had a lot of jobs in my 57 years. I always feel like she values me as a person first, then as her trusted colleague. She loves finding out about yet another skill I have that I hadn't mentioned earlier—usually because I'd forgotten about it too. I always go home in an up mood, because I know I did well at work."

It was no accident that Sandy ended up in her dream job. After taking several series of tests, she realized she was a Jill of all trades stuck in a one-skill job. She needed a lot more variety to put all her assets to good use. So when she heard about this position, she knew it would be the prefect fit for her.

> **Remember, besides knowing what kind of job you want to go after, it's equally useful to know which kind of job you *don't* want to do.**

These two areas of improvement—communication and interpersonal skills—are critical for developing your leadership abilities. Ignoring weaknesses in those areas will leave you with a high probability for failure in a leadership assignment—not the destination anyone wants!

FIXING COMPETITION GAPS: Yes, Virginia, you do have to run a race

Basically this stage consists of taking what you learned from this exercise (Page 117) and adding any gaps you discover to their appropriate list (education, interpersonal, etc.). It's also good to include this information in an overview discussion with your mentor. For example, if the same items keep appearing in your job evaluations, in your feedback from your Faultfinder Mentor, in reports from selection

panels, then you have to ask yourself—can I afford to ignore this any longer?

What did you learn from your competition—what experience or training do they have that you don't—and is it worth pursuing too? That's the big question you have to answer as you study your Competition Gap Worksheet. While you can't always equal your competitors in all areas, look for patterns in your gap analysis. If the same or similar gap items keep recurring, then that's clearly a boulder that's rolling into your roadway. If you feel that's your story, then note what it is here.

_____

_____

_____

_____

_____

_____

_____

_____

_____

_____

_____

_____

_____

_____

_____

_____

_____

_____

_____

_____

Compass Point

Sometimes the feedback is tough to take, especially if it feels personal. If you keep hearing that you don't take direction well, or that you're hyper-critical and people don't want to work on projects with you, then that could be a wake-up call. Talk to some trusted friends and see if they agree. You may need to do some deep level soul searching to unlock the answers to those sorts of issues. You can always start with self-help books and DVDs. But if those aren't enough, consider moving on to counseling or hiring a life coach.

Sometimes we just develop poor life habits—whether it's eating too many Cheetos, sipping too many margaritas or failing to control your short temper at work. Ask that face in the mirror if you're really bringing your best self to work every day, or have you slipped into some questionable behavior patterns. Of course we all have off days. What I'm talking about is the overall impression you make on those around you week in and week out. If you want to know, **ask a few co-workers whose opinion you value how they'd rate your on-the-job attitude. Then ask them to rate the people you're competing against for that promotion you want.** See if their responses confirm your competition analysis.

Just about any bad habit can be managed, mitigated or repressed entirely (at least at work). Let's take anger management as an example. **Changing behavior is about the payoff you can expect.** What's more important to you? Blowing off steam at work by allowing inappropriate anger to get the best of you, or reining it in and presenting a professional demeanor that will earn you the kind of trust and advancement you desire? (Hey, you can always take a kick boxing class after work!)

WORKSHEET: Development Assignments To Fill Your Gaps

- What skill do you need to develop?

_____

_____

_____

_____

_____

- What kind of assignment would lead to that?

_____

_____

_____

_____

_____

- Who has the authority to give the assignment?

_____

_____

_____

_____

- How long should it take to learn that skill?

_____

_____

- Can your mentor facilitate such an assignment?

_____

- Can you meet with the manager in question to seek that assignment?

_____

_____

- What can you do to prepare for this assignment to insure your success?

_____

_____

_____

_____

_____

- How will you be remarkable when you take on this assignment? What extra effort can you make to do an outstanding job?

_____

_____

_____

- How will you get noticed (in a good way) for doing a great job?

_____

_____

_____

_____

- How will you document your progress and demonstrate that you've learned these skills?

_____

_____

_____

_____

- What preparations do you need to make in order to document your assignment?

_____

_____

_____

_____

_____

- Will you need additional assignments to master this skill?

_____

_____

_____

_____

- Where will those come from?

_____

_____

_____

_____

- What other skills could mastering this one push you toward? And where might *those* skills take you?

_____

_____

_____

_____

- Does your attitude need an adjustment? Or do you already see how this can be a fun journey, creating your best career possibilities?

_____

_____

_____

_____

FIXING SELECTION PANEL VISIBILITY GAPS: Here's your chance to make a second impression

Especially if you've been turned down by a selection panel in your organization, you need to revamp your strategy in this area. This can easily be the game changer for you. Consider these points:

- How can you get visibility with each person on the panel?

- Identify actions, assignments and presentations you can do to meet these people and communicate your talents to them.

- Work with your manager and mentor to get those types of assignments in order to gain the visibility you need.

- The more voters on a selection panel that know you and your capabilities, the better you will score in the selection process. It really is that simple. Trust me—been there on lots of panels, wrote this book about it!

Creating your Itinerary or Development Plan

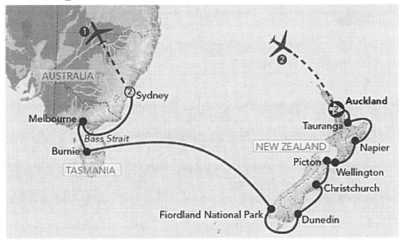

After meeting with your boss and your mentors and doing all the work of this chapter, document what you've agreed to do on your formal written development plan. Think of it as your travel itinerary, which details where you hope to go and when, as well as how long you hope to stay at each new destination. Get your Manager and Mentor to sign the plan. Every quarter meet with your manager and mentor to discuss your progress, problems that surface and changes you need to make to the plan. A sample plan follows on Page 154.

What if the job you want doesn't exist where you already work?

Maybe you need to design your own job! Yolanda had enjoyed much of the first 18 years of her career as a nurse on a busy inner city maternity ward. However, over the years, changes in hospital policies meant women no longer stayed more than a day on the ward, and Yolanda had lost all sense of connection to the new mothers and their babies. What had started out as a joyous job helping women adjust to their new roles as mothers, had become a factory situation with way too much paperwork. "The problem I saw was that first-time moms were terrified of being sent home only hours after delivery with very little information or support," she recalls. "It caused me so much anxiety, because here I was with all the answers they so desperately needed, but there was no time for me to share them."

This led her to start an outpatient education course for new moms and dads at her hospital. That went so well that Yolanda convinced the administration to let her expand the first class into a whole series of

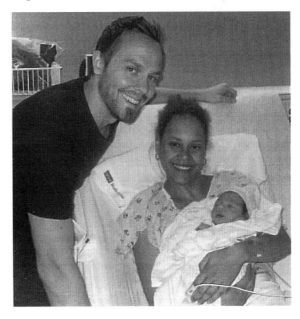

classes—and into a whole new job for herself. "Now I've come full circle, and I'm back doing what I loved about my old job—helping new mothers learn to care for their babies."

For Yolanda, the "aha" moment was realizing that patients still needed her expertise—all she needed to do was figure out a new way to give it to them. It was good for the hospital too, because offering the classes was a big selling point to expectant women choosing a hospital for their births. Yolanda saw a need and filled it and created a much better career for herself in the process.

Have there been changes in your company or industry that have left service gaps? Can you think of ways to fill them—making both you and your company look good in the process? Or are there other innovations that come to mind that you could suggest to management, with a view to creating a new position for yourself? Write your ideas below.

_____

_____

_____

_____

_____

_____

_____

_____

_____

_____

If you jump ship, be sure you know what's in the water

Wendy had to learn this the hard way. Wendy was thrilled with her job at a Los Angeles public relations firm, where she helped authors promote their books. "I love my job . . it has a lot of variety, and I feel like I'm learning something new every day," she confides. All that fit in nicely with her work style and love of attention to detail. All was well, until the firm's number one client asked her if she'd like to work for him exclusively. "He made me an offer I couldn't—but should have—refused. . . a huge salary increase and a $2,000 bonus for every speech I booked for him."

Wendy, who was saving for a down payment on a house, was seduced by the offer and left her wonderful job—even though there were tiny voices in the back of her mind trying to talk her out of it. She should have listened to them. After only six months, Wendy was begging for her old job back. So what happened?

"I had a hunch the new job would

require me to do things I didn't feel comfortable doing, but I kept hearing advice like 'Do what you fear and the money will follow' and so on. I really wanted to grow, so I decided to challenge myself. In truth, making the cold calls to book the author for speeches literally made me sick to my stomach—every time." Wendy hated sales, especially when she didn't know the clients. She just wasn't wired for it, and no matter how much she *wanted* to try it, she was never going to enjoy it or be great at it. **Will alone cannot overcome how you instinctively respond to situations.** That's why the sooner Wendy quit that job, the sooner her digestive tract was going to return to normal. As luck would have it, she got her old job back and threw out her antacids.

Tips For Overcoming Obstacles

Keys to working well with your HR Team

Because they are gatekeepers— among other things—people who work in Human Resources departments can seem intimidating. And because they have access to your personnel files, it can be instinctive to be wary of these folks. Additionally, they're often the ones who are involved with education vouchers and other perks, so they can wield a lot of power. **Which is why I'm encouraging you to see them as your allies.** If you work in a large organization, the HR department handles the flow of job openings, so they can be very helpful in that regard. Their influence varies from company to company, but these hardworking people can often make your life a lot easier. Here are a few suggestions:

✔ Get to know them—make a point of sitting next to them at lunch or company events.

✔ Be appreciative—send a real Thank You note if they help you out

✔ Seek their advice on certain aspects of your development plan

✔ Let them know you're ambitious and eager to grow in responsibility and skills

✔ Tell them you'd love to hear of any new training opportunities that arise

✔ Ask them which managers and executives *they* think are on the rise, people who might be good to get to know or work for directly

Once you get to know one or more people in this department, they can be ideal people to recommend a mentor or coach. And if you ever need an advocate to dispute some situation you may find yourself in, having laid genuine groundwork with someone in your HR department could pay off big time. Keep in mind, that most HR people have to walk a tightrope, as both representatives of the company and its policies and as champions for the employees. This sometimes puts them in difficult positions, which is why they also need your understanding. But they make fantastic allies should you need one.

Bon Voyage!

Whew! If you've made it this far in the workbook, filled out all these worksheets and met with your development team, then you should be ready to set sail on your great adventure—creating and thriving in a fulfilling career that brings your life much pleasure and a feeling a great accomplishment. As well it should. This is no easy task to reinvent yourself and to set off into uncharted territory. I hope I've been a good guide for you, but I'm not quite done with you yet.

• The next chapter includes my tips and checklists for how to be a world-class employee (and someone who's in high demand).

• The final chapter will show you how to continue to use this process throughout your entire career.

• At the back of the book you'll find some additional resources, including a reading list of other books that might help with specific issues you may have.

I wish for you a career as satisfying as the one I had. May you always find work to do that aligns with your values and inspires your passions. If you found this book useful, I'd love to hear your story. Please find me on Facebook at: carolynevanoff.

**Wishing you calm seas and fair winds,
Carol Evanoff**

SAMPLE Career Development Plan

Name: Samantha Jones
Date: 4/24/2011
Position: Accountant
Mentor: Carol Lee
Manager: Joe Smith

Career Goal Next Step: Accountant Sr.

Requirement Gap(s) in Education: Need Earned Value Management Training

* Corporate class 101-Mgr
* Earned Value Management Book

Work Experience Gap(s): Need to work an EVM Account Project K

* Assign Project K Cost Account

Competition Gap(s): Need presentation skills

* Corporate Class in Presentations 311P

Selection Panel Gap: Not know by Board Members

* Assign presentation to board meeting on Project K

Mentee Signature: _____

Mentor Signature: _____

Manager Signature: _____

SAMPLE Career Development Plan

Name: Jean White
Date: 4/24/2011
Position: Security Analyst
Mentor: Carl Evans
Manager: Craig Jones

Career Goal Next Step: Security Analyst Sr.

Requirement Gap(s) in Education: Complete Master's degree

* University of Washington Master's Thesis

Work Experience Gap(s): Need Top Secret Clearance

* Start Top Secret paperwork

Competition Gap(s): Need Investigation Training

* Corporate Class in Investigations-201I

Selection Panel Gap: Not know by Security Director

* Assign presentation to Security Director

Mentee Signature: _____

Mentor Signature: _____

Manager Signature: _____

CHAPTER EIGHT

How To Be A World-Class Employee

It's a whole new world now

For most people, the days of shuffling along in a so-so job with a mediocre attitude and middle-of-the-road performance record are over. The economic crisis that began in 2008 has altered the workplace mindset for everyone. (Or at least it *should* change how you feel about your job. Even holders of union jobs and tenured professors are seeing those once-secure positions erode.) **All companies now need to be lean in order to survive, and that means getting the most value from each and every employee.** If you don't want to become a statistic and join the legions of unemployed workers, you MUST rethink how you approach your career. The good news is, there are ways to more or less protect yourself from a sudden layoff. We'll examine them in this chapter.

It's the least favorite thing any manager has to do—give someone the terrible news that they're losing their job. No amount of empathy for the worker's family or economic plight will affect the decision. These days all managers must produce. Period. That means they're being held accountable for the profits or losses in their departments, and there just isn't any room for soft-heartedness. If a manager isn't ruthless, it'll be his head on the block next. So just because you get along great with your boss and you know he likes you, it's no guarantee you're the one he'll pick to keep when it's crunch time.

As someone who's had to make those tough choices, I can tell you that when someone clearly stands out as a stellar employee, I do everything I can to keep them employed.

Going with the premise that in a challenging economy any job is better than none, these are some compromises/changes you may need to make:

• Take a demotion as your manager shuffles multiple people into the best slots.

• Accept a promotion, even if you don't feel ready for it, with the accompanying stress and need to immerse yourself in your new position.

• Endure a pay cut and/or a reduction in benefits for performing the same job.

• Become more productive and take on more assignments—in short, do the work that used to take two people to accomplish.

• Start taking some of your work home with you.

• Do a lateral move to another department or facility, even if it means a longer commute or other hardships.

• Go through retraining for an entirely new position.

• Change your shift or schedule, perhaps to a flex-time situation.

• Reduce your hours and your resulting paycheck.

• Transfer to a different city or state.

While some version of these options may well be in your future, you can prepare for a better outcome. **The very best way to survive—and even thrive—these tough times is to become the STAR employee who retains the BEST job when all the dust settles.**

Performance is the key

First and foremost, your performance will speak to management louder than any mentor, boss or advocate. Employees who approach their job each day doing their very best and going above and beyond what's required are said to be *performing*. Workers who are clearly motivated are highly sought

after and are given the most opportunities to develop and advance. **Watch out for these potholes, which can affect your performance:**

1. Measuring your performance against your peers. Never stop aiming higher just because you're working at the same level as everyone else. That won't make your stand out in anyone's mind.

2. Believing when you get your assignments done that you don't need to ask for more work. It's people who keep asking for more who impress bosses the most.

3. Thinking you don't need to participate in the menial aspects of a project. People who can and do tackle the entire project are desired for high performing teams.

4. Procrastinating! Get it done now.

Learn ways of time management. Verify that your boss believes the assignment is complete.

5. Feeling you've arrived at a level of competency and you can coast from then on. Always strive to get better, faster and more productive. Understand continuous improvement is a way of life.

6. Keeping quiet. Volunteer! Step out of the shadows—be seen and heard. Continue to take on assignments to reach your performance potential.

7. Feeling you aren't personally responsible for your team's success. Work to make you AND your teammates successful.

8. Believing all that matters is your own career. Coach your peers, share good ideas. Pay it forward!

Three things I learned from Carol...

1. Don't try and be a glamour girl—everyone wants the glam jobs. Instead volunteer for those jobs that aren't so glamorous—where you have to dig in and get into the details. You won't be in competition with anyone for these jobs—and you could become an expert in that field.

2. Don't be a workaholic—working yourself to the point of burnout doesn't do anyone any good. Take a break, go for a walk, call a friend. When you come back to your project—you'll be refreshed and ready to tackle the job.

3. Don't work harder—work smarter. There's always room for improvement. Working harder on a project is not always the best answer. Instead, pull yourself away and take another view of how to approach your project. Become your own efficiency expert.

Keep asking yourself: How can I be amazing today? If you perform well, you'll have the opportunity to do so many other things that could make you happier. Great employees get noticed, complimented

and rewarded. They become role models for their teams. They receive perks and plum assignments. Their ideas and contributions are valued. When life intervenes (as it

Elizabeth is another star graduate of my mentoring program who avoided those potholes, and she was kind enough to share her insights on the process:

always does!) and you need a personal day off, you're far more apt to get it with a minimum of hassle if you've already proven yourself to be a star worker. **Best of all, when you make the effort to perform well, so many more options appear on your career map—and you get to pick which ones you want to visit.**

Gina's story is a good example of someone who turned her career—and her life around. She'd dropped out of college after a year, mostly because she hadn't found a course of study that ignited her. (And to be honest, following her boyfriend to another state had a lot to do with it, too.) She found herself taking the first job she was offered, again without finding something to do that fired her up. She'd been languishing in a warehouse job at a home improvement store for several years, getting more depressed as she saw her future

grow increasingly dim and gray. She knew education was one route out of the warehouse, but she wasn't motivated to even explore her options.

Finally, she allied herself with a new boyfriend who recognized her potential (a mentor in disguise!) and encouraged her to take responsibility for her career. With his support, she took her first steps toward something better. After taking two night courses in horticulture, she discovered her true passion. Lucky for her, the center where she worked also has a garden department, and her management was willing to help out with her education in that field.

Today she manages that department, gets to be outdoors most of the time and is thrilled to be working with living plants (instead of boxes!). She's earning enough money to afford a house, and her company even has a matching plan that helps with the down payment. **But none of this would have happened if Gina hadn't taken full responsibility for her own career and taken steps to change it.**

WORKSHEET: What An Employee Can Do
Attitude Checklist

Check off ones you've mastered and circle ones that still need work.

- Think and behave ethically.
- Take responsibility for your career.
- Always perform to *your* potential, don't gauge your performance against group averages—average is NOT a good thing!
- Stay positive, even in tough times.
- Plan, plan, plan! Keep referring back to your Development Plan. Never stop growing in education or experience.
- Take the initiative in your pursuit of your objectives. Don't wait for some magic fairy to help you. You can ASK for help, but YOU need to be proactive about it.
- Feel good about yourself when you see yourself overcoming hurdles and moving on to the next level of difficulty.
- Take chances, do the tough assignments.
- Be prepared to make suggestions.
- Build a tool box of skills by imitating qualities of successful people you respect. Discard methods that don't work for you.
- Practice active listening and rephrase key points to ensure the message you're receiving is the one that's intended.
- Treat people with respect and dignity—just as you'd want to be treated.
- Show that you value other's contributions and input. Ask for advice in their area of expertise. Give people credit for their contributions.
- Praise your co-workers when warranted. Empathize with them.
- Approach things positively and constructively. Nobody likes a naysayer.
- Understand and be loyal to your organization's objectives.
- Celebrate successes—socializing with co-workers can be a bonding experience.

NOTES

_____
_____
_____
_____
_____
_____
_____
_____
_____
_____
_____
_____
_____
_____
_____
_____
_____
_____
_____
_____
_____
_____

Teresa had a lot of bad habits when I first met her. Her home life was a mess and she brought all those problems with her to work. She was in an abusive relationship where she felt powerless, so work was the one place where she could vent her anger. She was hyper-critical and snapped at her team members over the slightest conflict. Her personnel file was bulging with complaints, and she'd been shuffled from one department to another as managers dumped her from their teams. Teresa was one fit of rage away from being fired, and she didn't even realize it.

After I heard her story, I felt she could be helped, so I connected her to a group who works with abused women, counsels them and ultimately helps them leave their abusers. Then I decided to show Teresa her file and the stack of complaints it contained.

She needed a jolt to shake up her pattern of behavior. With two kids to support and the prospect of becoming a single parent, she soon got on board with a program of self-improvement. **The self-esteem she gained as she reclaimed control of her life and her destiny was profound to witness.**

Five years later, she's advanced to management and is becoming someone other women go to for advice on *their* problems. She's a compassionate manager, because she knows all too well the challenges of work/life balance. As she explains, "Having a safe place to tell my story was the turning point. It's so hard to see your way out of a horrible situation on your own. I stayed in counseling for two years because it helped me so much. Now I love my job, and best of all I love helping other women transform their lives, too."

RECLAIM YOUR LIFE!

WORKSHEET: What An Employee Can Do
Education & Training Checklist

Check off ones you've mastered and circle ones that still need work.

• Be aware of all your company's employee development courses, and put in requests to attend at least one course every year.

• Join organizations such as the National Management Association and be an active member to increase your visibility.

• Keep updating your Education Plan, and make sure your education is consistent with your career goals.

• Use your company's tuition reimbursement program.

• Take advantage of any flex-time or comp-time options to allow for class attendance.

• Attend seminars and classes when they are available at your workplace.

• Take specialized classes to improve your writing, negotiating and presentation skills.

• Watch for other opportunities to advance specialized skills, whether in sales, accounting, systems design, etc.

• Stay current with all the latest software in your field—don't rely on your IT guys to bail you out all the time. Be the one everyone else asks for help—that will be noticed.

• Read books, magazines, trade journals, blogs and anything you can find that's relevant to your industry.

• Think ahead—ask your supervisor if she knows of any changes on the horizon you could be preparing for.

• Develop your own skills as a trainer, as it demonstrates leadership. Take an intern under your wing.

NOTES

_____

_____

_____

_____

_____

_____

_____

_____

_____

_____

_____

_____

_____

_____

_____

_____

_____

_____

As the oldest of six kids, Orice knew how to manage groups of people. She figured that aiming for a management level position would be a good fit for her, and she was on her way toward that goal. She began with sit-in assignments for supervisors. However, she wasn't finding them particularly fulfilling. It wasn't really the right match for her personality, but she couldn't figure out why.

And then one day at my urging, she volunteered to let a new hire shadow her around for a week. A lot of people run screaming from that scenario, but Orice blossomed almost immediately. Teaching others was second nature to her, and the feeling of helping younger people brought back plenty of good memories and emotions from her childhood. Before I knew it, she was down in the HR department begging to learn how to become a full-time trainer for the company.

Six months later she got her wish, and she's never looked back. She even passed up a chance to become a manager in the training department, because she's clear that for now, at least, staying active as a teacher is what fires her up every morning and makes her feel great about her career.

Be aware of software needs

I doubt there are many jobs these days that don't rely to some extent on computers and knowing various software programs. For those of you who are naturally techy, that's probably the fun aspect of your job. For the rest of you, it may range from a challenge to a royal pain in the you know what.

I have a news flash for you: computers are here to stay. And so is software. And just when you've mastered a program, there's always a new update with another learning curve. Plus it probably seems like there's always another new program to learn.

Regardless of your current attitude about that, I'm here to tell you how to make software your new best friend and use it for your own personal advantage.

DEMONSTRATE LEADERSHIP!

If you think learning software is unpleasant, imagine how your boss feels, knowing she needs to see that her entire department is up to speed. Software skills are so integral to today's workplace that it pays off tremendously to master your programs. First of all, it saves you time, allowing you to be more productive and be the star I'm always going on about. Second, it allows you to be helpful to your straggling teammates and earn points that way. Third, it provides a platform for you to shine, to be noticed, to be rewarded.

No matter how you *used* to feel about software, I dare you to ask your boss what NEW software would be helpful for you to learn and also what new programs are heading your way in the near future. Offer to be the first one on your team to try it out and to take some online training. That could be one huge burden removed from your supervisor's shoulders. And you know what else? That attitude demonstrates leadership and shows that you're growing into management material yourself!

If you really hate software, please consider this: do you hate it because you're not good at it? If so, maybe you just need to invest a few evenings in doing some tutorials or online classes. Check out YouTube—there are videos on there about using every kind of software imaginable.

For extra credit, if you work at a small company without a resident geek or IT department, then you might become the one who researches new software and efficiency applications that you can recommend to your boss. Set up an iGoogle home page with feeds of all the latest tech news, and you'll be the first kid on the block to know what's new and handy. Your boss may just build a shrine to you if you're good at this!

WORKSHEET: Software Mastery

Make an accurate and thorough list of every program you know in the space below. Check the appropriate column to indicate your level of competency. (Do NOT pretend to be a whiz at something when you're not.)

Programs I'd like to learn:

- Then in the space following this list, note what other programs you'd like to learn so you can research how to get training in them.
- Also note any other programs that you expect to have to learn in the coming months.
- Keep a copy of this worksheet in your personnel file and your passport.

PROGRAM	ZERO	SOME	GOOD	TOPS
⎯⎯⎯⎯⎯⎯	⎯	⎯	⎯	⎯
⎯⎯⎯⎯⎯⎯	⎯	⎯	⎯	⎯
⎯⎯⎯⎯⎯⎯	⎯	⎯	⎯	⎯
⎯⎯⎯⎯⎯⎯	⎯	⎯	⎯	⎯
⎯⎯⎯⎯⎯⎯	⎯	⎯	⎯	⎯
⎯⎯⎯⎯⎯⎯	⎯	⎯	⎯	⎯
⎯⎯⎯⎯⎯⎯	⎯	⎯	⎯	⎯
⎯⎯⎯⎯⎯⎯	⎯	⎯	⎯	⎯
⎯⎯⎯⎯⎯⎯	⎯	⎯	⎯	⎯
⎯⎯⎯⎯⎯⎯	⎯	⎯	⎯	⎯
⎯⎯⎯⎯⎯⎯	⎯	⎯	⎯	⎯
⎯⎯⎯⎯⎯⎯	⎯	⎯	⎯	⎯
⎯⎯⎯⎯⎯⎯	⎯	⎯	⎯	⎯
⎯⎯⎯⎯⎯⎯	⎯	⎯	⎯	⎯
⎯⎯⎯⎯⎯⎯	⎯	⎯	⎯	⎯
⎯⎯⎯⎯⎯⎯	⎯	⎯	⎯	⎯
⎯⎯⎯⎯⎯⎯	⎯	⎯	⎯	⎯

Programs I'd like to learn:

_____

_____

_____

_____

_____

_____

_____

Programs I may train in soon:

_____

_____

_____

_____

_____

WORKSHEET: What An Employee Can Do
Experience Checklist

Check off ones you've mastered and circle ones that still need work.

• Seek out challenging assignments with greater responsibility, but also assess the risks that go with them.

• Actively pursue development of a career plan and ask for regular feedback every 3-6 months, not just annually.

• Volunteer for company sponsored task forces, especially if you're interested in the issue. This is a great way to meet people at higher levels on the organization chart.

• Request lateral job rotations, swap jobs with someone, urge your manager to sponsor cross-training.

• Ask for rotational assignments even if they're outside of your area of expertise— that's how you test other areas of interest to see if they're a good fit for you, and that's how you grow.

• Apply for job rotations into new departments with assistance of your manager and mentor.

• Grab every opportunity to present your work. Always be prepared to do so, and do it professionally and with flair. (Remember, you want to be amazing!)

• Continue development in your area of expertise. Be personally responsible for staying current in all technical areas.

• Insure your performance is always excellent. If your performance is not superior, understand why—and do something about it.

• Know your talents and look for ways to use them.

• Look for opportunities to assist peers and supervisors in your area of expertise.

• Track your action items, conditions of satisfaction, and delivery times. Deal with all loose ends. That's a surefire route to becoming your manager's favorite.

• Research new projects fully and know what's expected of you. Don't fake answers. "I don't know, but I'll find out" is an acceptable response. Ask questions when you don't know what you're doing.

• Request development opportunities that can lead to advancement: in planning, problem-solving skills and budget management.

• Always manage your budgets (both

money and time).

- Look for opportunities to be valuable to your organization—be an innovator.
- Know the limits of your authority and who to go to when approvals are needed.
- Broaden your experience base in all directions, not just vertically.

Kristen's story really makes me smile because the outcome is so unexpected—and yet it derives from her own efforts. Kristen was yet another bored employee marking time in the back office of a huge car dealership. Her days consisted of processing contracts and mailing out appointment reminders. She'd been given an opportunity to move into sales, but knew she wasn't cut out for that. She enjoyed the people she worked with, her commute was just five minutes and her benefit package was decent, so **she was afraid to rock the boat** by looking for another job that might be worse.

Then one day in the lunchroom she heard one of the managers talking about

setting up accounts on YouTube and Twitter and trying to use them to drive customers to their dealership. Kristen's ears perked way up, because she was a master of social media and could immediately determine that these guys were clueless.

> **So she joined the conversation and displayed her knowledge of social media by whipping out her iPhone and showing them videos she'd made and uploaded to YouTube as well as her various other accounts.**

As she recalls, "I tried not to come off as smug, but you should have seen their faces. You'd have thought I showed them the Mona Lisa or something."

Within a few months Kristen had been promoted to Social Media Marketing Manager and spent most of her time making really fun videos, featuring shiny new cars driving to fun destinations around town. She came up with contest ideas. She tweeted fun incentives like: *Today's John's b'day—buy a car from him & you get to throw a cream pie at him!* Her efforts were so successful that sales shot up and she started connecting her own bonuses to her videos, which is paying off handsomely. **She's been approached by several other dealerships who want her on their team, but she's remaining loyal to the company that gave her a chance to utilize her talents.** So what hidden talents can you bring into the light?

WORKSHEET:
Harnessing My Talents

Make a thorough list of all your skills and special talents, arranging them in likely groups. List things even if you can't imagine how they might be used at work.

★ Rank them on a scale from 1-10 according to how much joy you get when utilizing that talent.

★ Put a checkmark next to ones you are currently using at work, and circle ones that you'd like to be using more.

★ What jumps out at you? If there are lots of things on your list that are remaining hidden or being wasted, then discuss this list with your mentor and see how to apply this information to your development plan.

SPECIAL SKILLS & TALENTS   JOY RANK

_____ _____

_____ _____

_____ _____

_____ _____

_____ _____

_____ _____

_____ _____

_____ _____

_____ _____

_____ _____

_____ _____

_____ _____

_____ _____

_____ _____

_____ _____

_____ _____

_____ _____

_____ _____

_____ _____

_____ _____

WORKSHEET: What An Employee Can Do
Networking Checklist

Check off ones you've mastered and circle ones that still need work.

• Exercise networking opportunities in a positive and constructive manner to learn and become better known inside and outside your company.

• Develop a network across organizations you join.

• Develop a personal/professional network and stay connected via social media (just be sure to keep it professional!)

• Ask for help via social media—you'll be astounded at how much perfect strangers want to help you. You can ask for job leads, coaching referrals, skill training sources—anything really.

• Post in online forums for help with all phases of career development. Just Google "career forums" or "career development forums" for a start.

• Join professional associations and be active in them, such as the IAAP, the International Association of Administrative Professionals. There's a group out there for nearly every job description.

• Share your vision for success with people you meet. You never know when some random meeting can lead to an incredible opportunity. But the helpful stranger can't help you if you don't tell the world what you need and want.

• Form or join a mastermind group, especially if you have really big dreams or equally big challenges. You can learn all about them online, but basically it's a small group of people with similar goals who meet regularly to support one another's progress however they can. If having more people to be accountable to is a tactic that works well for you, then this could be the ticket to your fabulous future.

• Go to class reunions and alumni events—those are classic networking opportunities, as people are often motivated to help those with ties to the same schools.

• Become more social in your personal life. Especially if you're invited to a function by someone from work, by all means accept and be prepared to give a 30-second pitch for who you are and where you're aiming.

That last item is so important, I'm going to say some more about it. Even if

you're a classic wallflower by nature, you need to get over it on business occasions and any social situation where you might meet influential people. **You'll be asked thousands of times in your life what you do for a living.** Which response do you think could lead to something exciting?

1. Oh, I'm just a secretary in the billing office at Acme Construction.

2. Currently I work at Acme Construction, but I'm taking night classes in estimating and I spend my free time visiting job sites. I'd really like to become a contractor or perhaps a home inspector. I'm looking for apprentice positions now.

Same question:

1. I run an industrial sewing machine making sails for boats.

2. I work at the boat haven, and I'm learning everything there is to know about outfitting high-end sailboats. I hope to expand that knowledge with hands-on experience crewing on a large boat this summer with a view toward getting into boater education or perhaps being a docent on an historical ship.

See how the second choices tell you

exactly where she wants to go? That way, if the person you're speaking with *does* have any connections in those areas, they'll be apt to help you out. **So don't be afraid to tell your story—just practice keeping it short and fascinating.**

For an example of how networking can make you a star at work, meet Gloria, who works as an administrative assistant to the owner of a mortgage brokerage in Oregon. Because of what she learned working there, she was able to buy her first home. However, in her popular area, real estate prices have remained strong in the last few years, leaving many people on the sidelines believing they no longer qualify as home buyers. Gloria knew this, because many of her friends were floundering in that boat, so **she came up with a plan to offer free classes in home buying along with a free evaluation of financial readiness**. Her theory was that if people liked her classes, they would naturally be inclined to apply for loans through her company, which specialized in helping people with less than stellar credit obtain mortgages.

"My boss loved the idea, so I immediately set out to make all the arrangements," Gloria explains. "Through my contacts at the chamber of commerce, I was able to secure a good location for the classes, and a friend who's a teacher agreed to coach me on my course outline and presentation. Another friend helped me design flyers for the class. Word began to spread about the classes, and we had people calling to register before we even announced them. The real bonus for me is that it fulfills my deep need to help people get homes of their own."

This is a great example of how you might network to put the pieces of your project in place. Gloria had never designed a flyer, but she had a friend who knew how. Nor had she ever taught a class, but she knew someone who taught for a living. Instead of seeing obstacles, Gloria figured

out what she needed to make happen to enable her vision.

WORKSHEET: What An Employee Can Do
Be Coachable Checklist

Check off ones you've mastered and circle ones that still need work.

(As a quick refresher, this isn't about training, which is learning new skills. This is about improving your performance over time and achieving better results.)

• Always request a debriefing after going through a selection process, whether or not you got the job. (Just as you need to know why you don't get a job, it's also useful to know which aspects of your career passport and interview clinched the deal for you.) Just frame your request as part of your self-improvement mission.

• Be open even if you disagree with the outcome of selection process.

• Don't believe everything someone tells you about your performance, especially a co-worker who may have ulterior motives. Analyze the feedback and confirm in your own mind if it makes sense.

• Seek honest performance feedback, not just obligatory comments. Ask for details, examples.

• Try not to be defensive when a supervisor singles you out for criticism. If you don't understand how to improve, ask for more direction.

• Practice your communication skills and deliberately watch yourself doing it.

• Make personal assessments. Ask others to observe and participate in the assessment process.

• Accept that you may make mistakes in the process of learning and don't beat yourself up about it.

• Acknowledge that you will learn by these mistakes.

• Take it a step at a time. Successful communicators are not made overnight. It takes initiative, basic skill knowledge, and practice, practice, practice.

• Be willing to learn and change. Be open to becoming more engaged, more involved in your company's mission.

• Learn to be a true team player. If this is tough for you, read up on it. This is a skill like any other that can be learned. See the book list on Page 193 for help.

Bonita decided that at age 45, she'd wasted enough of her life in crappy jobs, so she was highly motivated to turn her career around. She sought out the best mentors and coaches she could find and took all their advice to heart. A big issue that was uncovered for her was learning to be more focused at work and become more efficient. Now that so many people work at computers with internet access, the temptation to stray off and check your email or tweet a pal or shop for a birthday present can be difficult to repress. That's one of the bad habits Bonita had developed. **So she printed up the following card and pasted it on her monitor where she couldn't miss it.**

• Is this the best use of my time?

• How does this activity make a client more satisfied?

• How does this task contribute to the bottom line?

• Is there an easier way to accomplish this?

• Should I ask for help on this task?

Now she's on her sixth or seventh revision of the sign, having long since mastered the original problem. **This is being open to coaching and putting it into action.**

What similar reminders could you place around your work area? Besides being a useful tool, when your manager sees those signs, they're an indication of your commitment to improvement and how seriously you take your job.

Jot down any ideas for reminder signs here:

_____

_____

_____

_____

_____

_____

_____

_____

_____

_____

_____

_____

_____

_____

_____

- You can turn this loss into a situation where doors will open that might not necessarily be opened any other way.

- You can play the guilt card. Sadly, managers often rank female candidates second in the selection process. This can be a result of the "good old boy" network. If you suspect that's at play in your case, you can use his guilt to convince him to give you opportunities to do assignments for him. He may even be willing to mentor you. With that increased visibility, he'll be less likely to shortchange you the next time around.

Overcoming obstacles: losing selections

Let's talk about leveraging losses. What I learned early on in my career was that when you actually lose a selection you shouldn't miss out on the opportunity to try to leverage that loss to your benefit. The loss benefits you in several ways:

- You can meet with the manager who had the opening and find out where they saw some gaps in your experience.

- You get an opportunity to ask that manager for if he or she is willing to mentor you or offer you an opportunity to do is sit in assignments during vacations.

WORKSHEET: What An Employee Can Do
Working With Management Checklist

Check off ones you've mastered and circle ones that still need work.

- Make sure your boss recognizes your contributions. Find professional ways of doing this that don't make you come off as a kiss-up or bragger. Just state that you've taken care of XYZ assignment, as she requested. The fewer people who are present when you do this, the more likely you are to avoid being seen as an antagonist by your peers.

• Ask your boss what education or training would be beneficial to your career.

• Be certain your boss knows you value your job, that you're happy to have it and are committed to doing well at it. That may seem obvious, but you'd be surprised how seldom that sentiment gets expressed.

• Contribute your ideas and enthusiasm— your boss wants to know you're involved.

• Trust your management and don't participate in name calling, boss bashing or any kind of trash talking. Someone always squeals, and you end up looking like what you are—someone with a bad attitude!

• Actively seek measurements of your job performance results. You must know realistically how your performance stacks up against your peers.

• Then ask for coaching to make improvements. Few things warm a boss's heart more than an employee who *asks* for coaching!

• If relevant, find ways to add value in your interactions with customers—and to let your boss know you place a priority on client relations.

• Publicly acknowledge supervisor or manager support when appropriate. If you

receive a compliment for a team effort, include the others in your response.

• When your supervisor compliments you, be gracious and let her know what it means to you to be acknowledged. For some people, this is incredibly important. If that sounds like you, then let management know how much that inspires and motivates you.

• Look for opportunities to sit in for your boss. Learn what's important to your boss's boss. That perspective may be very revealing about how your department is run.

• Use that knowledge to look for areas you can improve or places to innovate new solutions to ongoing problems.

• Demonstrate a willingness to make appropriate decisions without being micro-managed.

• Offer to go the extra mile to solve a crisis—just don't let it become a regular thing. You deserve to be treated with respect and to be properly compensated for your time. If you're a salaried employee with the expectation of lots of take-home work, then it will be up to you to negotiate a fair balance. You can't work 16-hour days repeatedly and expect to have any kind of life.

• Look for activities that will foster two-way trust and respect. Being reliable is a great start.

• Seek opportunities to interface at higher levels in your organization.

- Obtain agreement with boss on your development plan.

- Show your boss that you can manage your time well and don't need a lot of hand-holding and supervision. Becoming great at time management is an incredibly valuable tool that will serve you well in all areas of your life.

- Follow company rules and policies, but (if needed) also let your boss know you expect him to do the same.

- If your supervisor isn't good about giving clear instructions, work with him to figure out a better way to communicate them. Could he sketch what's needed or demonstrate the task? Can he draw a map or show you examples of similar completed projects? Don't suffer in silence, expecting to let him down because you're unsure what's expected.

- Get commitments for training reimbursement, and give your boss updates on your educational progress. She'll want to know you're gaining something from the experience—especially if she went to bat for you in order to make it possible.

- Try and make a point of exchanging at least a few minutes conversation every week with your boss—whether on a personal or work-related topic. You need to keep the lines of communication wide open.

- Do your very best to get along with your supervisor. However, if after you've given it your all, the two of you are just like oil and water, then it can benefit you both to request a transfer to another department if that's a possibility. Consult your mentors for advice on how to navigate this sticky situation. Life's too short, though, to endure a work situation that's highly unpleasant.

Carla is a great case in point. Though she adored the actual work she did as a reporter at her small town newspaper, her boss was literally making her sick. She spent all her extra income on therapy, massages and anti-depressants just to able to keep working. **For unknown reasons, her boss failed to recognize how hard Carla was working** and became convinced she was goofing off whenever she was away from the office. He continued to pile more and more assignments on her, then still complained that she wasn't working hard enough. Finally she had to create a spreadsheet that detailed the number of column inches she was contributing each week in comparison to other reporters. (There's that power of documentation again!) Yet even that black and white proof didn't change his attitude. For whatever reason, her boss had it in for her, so after three years of losing that battle, Carla decided to give up the fight.

Since it was a small paper, there was no other department to transfer to, but Carla couldn't afford to just up and quit. She did, however, manage to find a great replacement for herself and make her boss think it was *his* idea. It took some adept maneuvering, but her boss became so eager to employ the new person that he allowed Carla to be laid off for medical reasons—which meant she could get unemployment benefits while she looked for a less stressful job.

So the moral of this story is: **work hard and document it, but if you aren't appreciated and you're wildly unhappy, then get the heck out of Dodge and move along.** I bet you can find a sunnier destination on your career journey.

WORKSHEET: What An Employee Can Do
Records Checklist

Check off ones you've mastered and circle ones that still need work.

• Take advantage of, and treat seriously, the company's recognition processes (performance appraisals, awards, commendations, employee development plans, etc.). Always make sure a copy is put in your personnel folder and keep a copy at home for your career passport.

• Prepare a thorough resume and have it put in your personnel files and use it in your discussions.

• Keep track of your performance highlights during the year and document them in your passport.

• Make arrangements to review your personnel folder/records. Make a checklist of what to look for, things that might be missing, such as: education documents, employee evaluations, commendations, awards, current resume, etc.

• Check job postings regularly. You never know when a whole new position may be created that fits you perfectly. Don't forget to look online, too.

• Update your development plan and resume yearly.

• Take careful notes at your performance review; note new tasks, paying close attention to detail and asking plenty of questions.

• Write your objectives carefully to document your planned accomplishments.

How NOT to do this!

Thomas is a military guy who had a blind spot when it came to this topic. Thomas came to us after 20 years in the Navy, and he met with me for some career counseling. I gave him this workbook to help him prepare for upcoming job openings.

So I was surprised when I learned that he failed to get the first position he went after, because I knew he was well qualified. The manager with the opening said his résumé didn't reflect that he was qualified, so he didn't think Thomas had the experience for the job.

When Thomas came in to see me afterward, **he admitted he hadn't done any of the worksheets or created his career passport.** He hadn't even updated his resume, which was a no-brainer for someone switching careers. I told him the main reason he didn't get the job was because his

military job titles were incomprehensible to private sector managers. I recommended he convert those job titles into the kinds of work and functions that he performed, so that his skills could be seen as easily transferable to these other jobs.

After TWO more rounds of selection failures because he would not do this work, Thomas finally sat down and did what I'd asked him to do all along. **When he applied for the next position he got it.**

It is interesting to me how some people feel like it's too much of a chore to use this workbook. They feel it's very labor-intensive, so they have a difficult time seeing the return on the time invested. But they also fail to realize it's especially important if you're changing jobs between companies, moving across functional organizations or shifting from the military to a non-military job. Not everybody uses the same terminology, and many industries use so much specific jargon that resumes must be translated into more universal language.

There can be big differences from one workplace to another, and that's where the career passport really pays off, because you can break down your job history into tasks and the kinds of work you've done, which is more easily communicated to the hiring manager.

The first month is really doing the facts gathering, collecting all your resume data, your past performance evaluations, job descriptions and schooling information. This is when you'd create your career passport in is as much detail as you can. This passport becomes the foundation for the analysis you need to do and the strategic thinking you'll need to do.

That will all lead to your filling in the gaps in your career to make you better able to compete for prized jobs. **I, for one, am sure you're worth it!**

So are YOU worth the time?

If you're dragging a bit on really jumping into this process, think about it: are you worth it, are you worth putting in the time and the energy to layout your detailed experience, identify your education and the jobs you've done in your career?

If you believe you're worth it, then you need to take the time to go through this process.

I think you wouldn't be reading this book if you didn't already believe to some degree that you're worth investing energy and time in building your career. Just know this process does take some time…typically I would guide someone through this process over the course of two to three months.

CHAPTER NINE
Tips For The
Rest Of Your Trip

Documenting your progress with this process

If you're reading this chapter, then you're either very thorough or you're moving along in this process to create your ultimate career journey. Either way, good for you! In fact, only a small percentage of people ever finish reading the books they acquire, so pat yourself on the back. The point of this brief chapter is to give you encouragement for the long haul, strategies for the rest of your career.

With most of the people I mentored, **they usually got their first promotion very quickly**, because they were already qualified and just needed to demonstrate that better in their passport. After that, however, it can take awhile to reach the next destination on your journey. That's normal, so don't feel you're failing somehow if you don't experience the fabled meteoric rise. Sure, in some industries if you get lucky you can ride a wave of innovation or expansion more quickly than in other companies, but a sure and steady rise is the norm. (And it's a lot easier to live through—meteoric rises are overrated—just ask any Hollywood star who burned out at 22 from too much too soon.)

Did a new road project leave you stranded?

Your biggest problem may well be complacency. Once you attain a level of success and satisfaction, it's human nature to want to kick back and enjoy life. That's cool. But like the small town that gets forgotten when the new freeway bypasses it, your career can fade into the background of daily life as you succumb to more and more obligations.

To offset that tendency, some of my most successful mentees make a habit of taking a solo weekend getaway every six months just to review their development plans, their personal and career goals and assess how they're doing. It's a good time to get caught up on reading in your industry, or even better, dip into some books that inspire and motivate you. There's something magical about a change of scene that forces you to view your life differently.

This is your retreat, so design it

however you think would be the most productive.

✔ One woman likes to take a roll of butcher paper and draw big flow charts.

✔ Another takes a box of colorful pens, pretty notebooks and silly stickers just to make her personal journaling process more fun and stimulating.

✔ A third likes to stay at a high-end resort, be totally pampered and make time

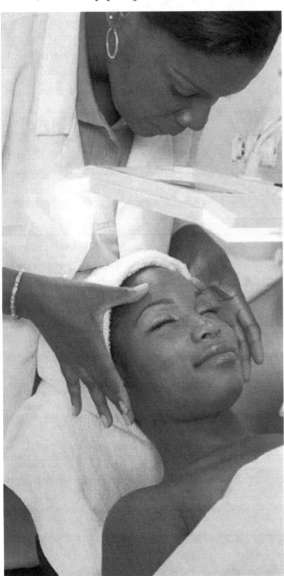

for spa treatments. All that nurturing is a reward she gives herself for her consistent hard work, and being able to really relax allows her mind to open up to new ideas.

If getting away just isn't feasible, you can always **plan a staycation.** Send the family away and stay home alone and indulge yourself in a weekend of focusing on nothing but you and your career. Play *your* music. Eat *your* favorite foods. Stay up late; sleep in. Make a mess. Scream. Shout. Dance. Shake your life up somehow. You'll be shocked at how much renewal you can attain with this method.

A cautionary tale

Meet Jessica, someone who went through this process and won her first few promotions then sort of forgot what she'd learned. She stopped updating her passport and her resume. She fell behind in software training. She got a little sloppy with her work habits and her productivity eroded as a result. **The wake-up call was when she went after a great opportunity and wasn't chosen.** That's when she returned to me to try and understand why.

No one wants to hear that they've slipped and aren't performing well. The signs were there in her evaluations, but she chalked them up to a supervisor she didn't particularly like. Jessica left my office defiant, still unwilling to believe that a few minor shifts in her behavior had cost her the plum job she really wanted. I made a point of speaking with the selection panel, and I know for a fact that's why she lost the promotion.

I gave her a few weeks to digest this news then called her back in for a follow-up chat. This time the former go-getter version of Jessica showed up, and she told me rather sheepishly that she had been slacking off, but didn't want to admit it to herself. As she told

me, "I'm not that person who adds five minutes to every coffee break, who takes long lunches, who calls in sick just because I don't feel like showing up. **Yet my behavior hasn't been in sync with my values.** I used to have a great work ethic, but lately I've been so pressured at home that I think of work as a place to relax and recover from my life—isn't that terrible?"

I assured her that it was just human, and a common reality at that. I also told her that while she might be able to coast awhile longer, eventually she'd be putting her job at risk if her performance didn't improve. So we worked out a plan to get her back on track.

I found her a new mentor to hold her accountable and they had regular check-ins every Monday and Friday. Within a few months, Jessica bounded into my office all smiles, excited about a new opening she was going to seek. I gave her my support, and yes, she got it.

For some people (myself included) **continually going after and learning a new position is what keeps us excited** and motivated to do our best. If you need that kind of incentive, too, then learn from Jessica and don't let your performance slide—and take you with it.

Stay out of the ruts!

Sometimes we can get stuck on an upward trajectory that isn't good for us. Yes, I wrote *upward*. If you missed the part about shaping your career like a pyramid rather than the proverbial ladder, then read it here: Page 109. If each new promotion is in the exact same department, working with the same products, clients, vendors and co-workers, **all that sameness can become**

numbing—no matter how much you enjoy it. A stimulating sideways move will snap you out of your doldrums and challenge you to start learning new things again. I've seen it happen over and over, so much so that I can flat out guarantee it works.

Sometimes promotions aren't the issue, it's just simple boredom. Sharee was in rut, but she didn't realize how deep it was until she jumped out of it one day. She

performed competently as the administrative assistant for the ad sales department of a community newspaper in a large Midwest city. It was reasonably interesting work. The salespeople she served directly were usually out of the office, so she had a lot of autonomy. After several years, Sharee realized there wasn't much left for her to learn about her job and no real challenges to keep her interested in it.

Then one day, when she heard the office manager ask for a volunteer to help out with distribution because a driver had called in sick, she leapt at the chance to escape the office for the morning.

"To my surprise, I learned I loved delivering the papers," she says, her voice still full of excitement. Sharee got to get outdoors, she was able to talk with small business owners and gather feedback about the paper and she interacted with readers who were happy to see the latest edition arrive. When she got back to the office, she asked her boss if she could create the position of Distribution Manager of the paper—tasks the office manager had been reluctantly squeezing in to her duties. "My boss about fainted that anyone would want such a thankless job, but I was thrilled she agreed."

Sharee liked recruiting drivers and meeting with them on the loading dock, organizing better routes and getting out in the community to find more outlets to carry the paper. She found a good deal on used sidewalk vending boxes, repainted them herself and made a real believer out of her

boss. As a result of her efforts, the circulation of the paper nearly doubled within a year, and Sharee not only earned a hefty bonus, but her grateful boss tied a salary incentive to future circulation increases—all because she volunteered to try something new—something she knew nothing about and could not have conceived of doing if she hadn't dared to climb out of her rut.

Try something different—who knows where it'll lead you! If you can think of some other duties where you work that you'd be willing to at least try, list them here.

_____

_____

_____

_____

_____

_____

_____

_____

_____

_____

_____

_____

_____

_____

Climbing out of a rut

It can happen to anyone. You know what I mean—you got tired of running quarterly reports, so now you never even looked for a better way to represent the data. You've written the in-house newsletter for many years, and it just seems easy to keep doing it the same way. You know your job so well that you do, indeed, do it while half asleep some days. After one bad experience, you decided long ago that you're not a team player, so you never ask for—or offer—help on anything. As the old saying goes, the only difference between a rut and a grave is the depth. Don't let your dreams of a more adventurous career get sucked down into a rut—or a grave.

Sometimes all it takes are a few small changes to effect substantial change. **Try some of these ideas on for size.**

1. Challenge yourself every once in awhile. Don't always take the safe route. Are you a mouse in the corner at staff meetings? Try speaking up and see what happens.

2. Do something differently. Shake things up a little; maybe a fresh approach will keep you interested. Take a class. Try new software. Talk to someone from another department at lunch and find out what they do.

3. Ask for a new task. Doing exactly the same things week in, week out, would numb any mind. Trade tasks with a co-worker for a day. Take a vendor to lunch. Go on a sales call. Order supplies. Anything out of your ordinary.

4. Offer to help a co-worker who's overwhelmed. You never know what may come of it. You may find other duties you're well-suited for; you may build a personal ally; you may get points for being a good team member. Gee, you might even have fun!

5. Reverse your usual mode. If you usually work on projects alone, try working with a partner, or vice versa. You may be a born collaborator and not know it. Or you may discover you really prefer to be a lone eagle.

6. Reconnect with your passion. Why are you working there? What aspects of your job used to excite you? Can you revive those feelings?

Warning—bridge washed out ahead!

At the risk of driving you nuts, I have to remind you once again of the importance of **staying current with documenting your career—EVERY step along the way**. Every darn day talented people lose out on thrilling positions because they can't demonstrate what they've done at past jobs. This is especially crucial when you move

from company to company. Not only will the people doing the hiring be clueless about your former duties and accomplishments, they won't have easy access to your management or co-workers to learn more. And don't think you can rely on former supervisors and mentors to vouch for you. What happens if one of those key players in your life moves to Madagascar or retires or joins the Marines? You'll be out of luck, that's what.

> **Trust me, luck is not a strategy for your success.**

It's almost as if you never even held your former jobs—unless you can tangibly SHOW the nice people what you did, what you learned, how you grew in your position, what contributions you made to your company and so on. A few lines on a resume just isn't enough, not by a mile.

That's never more important than it is during economically challenging times, so please don't slip on this ongoing assignment. It's ten times harder to do after the fact and impossible to do as good a job at it later, than if you'd tackled the documentation in real time. If you need a refresher course on Documentation 101, head right here: Page 69.

Don't let success kill you

A certain amount of stress is a normal, even necessary part of life. (We have to stay in shape to outrun those mastodons!) But when your stress level escalates into the

stratosphere and your health, relationships and job performance are threatened, then it's time to focus on some coping skills. As with most things, being prepared in advance is always a better option. As you grow and develop in your career and take on more and more responsibilities, you need to add in an increasing amount of activities that offset your pressures. What you pick doesn't matter.

The litmus test is: does the activity relax you and take your mind off work?

Is it fun? Is it challenging in a different sort of way from your job?

BE CHALLENGED!

WORKSHEET: Taming the stress monster

• List at least ten activities you enjoy that would be classified as stress relievers.

• List ten more that you've never tried, but that sound like something you might like.

• Commit to making time each week to enjoy at least one item from these lists. Check off each week that you actually do this. As with all good habits, learning how to relieve stress takes practice. **The time to learn it is** *before* **a cardiologist makes it mandatory!**

STRESS RELIEVING ACTIVITIES

_____
_____
_____
_____
_____
_____
_____
_____
_____
_____
_____
_____

NEW IDEAS

_____
_____
_____
_____
_____
_____
_____
_____
_____
_____
_____
_____
_____

Are you ready to move to a foreign country?

By country I mean Management Land. Many workers eventually have to decide if they're going to cross the great divide and join the management side of the workforce. Depending on your field, it can be a smooth, upward move or an unsettling, life-altering mind shock. If you're escalating from administrative assistant to office manager and you've been paying attention, then it shouldn't be too big a leap. But if your transition also includes shifting departments or a move to another city, then whoa…you need to be sure you're ready for that.

Higher pay, better benefits, more power and prestige are all great, but not everyone enjoys managing other people or being accountable in a more demanding way for the bottom line. Of course, your mentors and management are there to guide you in this process—if it's an internal upgrade. **This is an ideal time to consult your Faultfinder Mentors.** They'll delight in telling you twenty reasons why it's a bad idea—and I urge you to give them all careful consideration.

• I've challenged myself with multiple sit-in assignments for management and believe I have a good idea of what it takes to be a good manager.

• I've taken specific leadership training and I found it stimulating—it made me want this even more.

• I believe I enjoy the respect of my peers and that my co-workers would agree I have management capabilities.

Where you may be in over your head is if you're thinking about making this big leap at another company—not something you want to discuss at the water cooler. This is where having at least one mentor outside your company really pays off. To help you make this critical decision, I'm including this checklist. But only you can score it. Only you know what level of discomfort you can live with.

WORKSHEET: Am I ready to be a manager?

Check all that apply to you.

• I'm well organized and always plan my life well ahead of time.

• I've already begun to study the art of management and am eager to test what I've learned.

• I enjoy working closely with lots of different people.

• I'm a problem solver; I don't mind when people share their issues with me, whether personal or professional.

• I have a history of taking the initiative—when I see something that needs doing, I rally the team and we get it done.

• I'm a self-starter, and I don't need someone else always spelling out what I need to do next.

• I have excellent communication abilities and rarely find myself apologizing or having to explain my way out of a jam.

• I have great people skills: I'm tactful, considerate and know how to treat diverse employees with fairness and sensitivity.

• I'm a good judge of people and believe I'd choose excellent team members.

• I know how to motivate people to

ARE YOU MOTIVATING?

achieve their best performance. I'm good at boosting team morale.

• Improving the performance of a team excites me; I'm always looking for ways to do things better, simpler, more efficiently.

• I have Big Picture vision—I understand how each task contributes to the larger whole.

• I'm willing to jump in and get my own hands dirty to help my team if needed. But I also recognize that if it becomes a pattern, then I need to figure out what I'm doing wrong.

• I'm able to make tough decisions, even firing someone if need be. I can discipline people if necessary.

• I appreciate the value of delegating tasks to the right people. I know I can't do this by myself.

• I'm happy to share credit for a job well done.

• I can juggle doing my own job, supervising my staff and being accountable to my own boss.

• I have my own management mentor team in place, and know where to go for quality advice.

• I'm skilled at stress management—I rarely miss my weekly coping activity.

• I'm prepared to work harder, work longer hours, give up some evenings and weekends to attend company events.

• I don't mind socializing with other company executives or entertaining clients.

• I will use my status to make greater contributions beyond my company to my larger community.

Total up the number of checkmarks, then multiply by four. There are 25 questions, so that's your percentage score. Of course there are always more questions you might ask yourself, but these cover most of the basics of becoming a manager. Only you know what score will give you the confidence to pursue this further. However, if the number is below 50%, you might want to go back and work on some of the items you didn't check.

WORKSHEET: Schedule for tracking your progress.

Schedule a formal sit-down at least every six months with your development team, either all together or individually, to be sure you're on track for the development tasks you've outlined. Check off meetings you had, circle ones you need to make happen.

_____

_____

_____

_____

_____

_____

_____

_____

_____

_____

_____

_____

_____

_____

_____

_____

What's your yardstick?

Determine for yourself what constitutes good progress. Is it the grades you attain in college classes? Is it the number of classes or certifications you complete? Is it the number of sit-in opportunities you get in a year? It doesn't matter what measurements you use to monitor your progress as long as they're meaningful to you and help you stayed focused and motivated.

Track your action items, conditions of satisfaction, and delivery times to be sure you're performing to your fullest capacity

_____

_____

_____

_____

_____

_____

_____

_____

_____

_____

_____

_____

_____

How do you define success for this next year? Update this list annually and check off the goals you achieve.

_____

_____

_____

_____

_____

_____

_____

_____

_____

What new skills do you hope to learn in the next year?

_____

_____

_____

_____

_____

_____

_____

_____

_____

What kind of opportunities do you want to create for yourself ths year?

_____

_____

_____

_____

_____

_____

_____

_____

_____

On a scale of 1-100 what's your current level of job satisfaction? Ask yourself every year and track whether it goes up or down—then take appropriate action.

_____

Update your career passport and resume

You must document your projects and accomplishments at least quarterly, but even better, monthly or as they occur. Write a memo about what you learned from significant projects and how they impacted the company. **This is no time to be shy!** If you did something great, spell it out here.

If you only take one reminder from this chapter, let it be this—put a small sign where you'll see it daily:

How will I be amazing today?

Recommended Reading

The 7 Habits of Highly Effective People
by Steven R. Covey

The 8th Habit: From Effectiveness to Greatness
by Steven R. Covey

Abilene Paradox and Other Meditations on Management
by Jerry Harvey

The Fifth Discipline: The Art and Practice of a Learning Organization
by Peter Senge

The Fifth Discipline Fieldbook: Strategies and Tools for Building a Learning Organization
by Peter Senge

The First 90 Days: Critical Success Strategies for New Leaders at All Levels
by Michael Watkins

First Break All the Rules: What the World's Greatest Managers Do Differently
by Marcus Buckingham and Curt Coffman

Influencer: The Power to Change Anything
by Kerry Patterson, Joseph Grenny, David Maxfield and Ron McMillan

Just Promoted! A 12-Month Road Map for Success in Your New Leadership Role
by Edward Betof and Nila Betof

The Minding Organization: Bring the Future to the Present and Turn Creative Ideas into Business Solutions
by Moshe F. Rubinstein and Iris R. Firstenberg

The Pygmalion Effect
Jeremy Blanchette

Refuse to Choose! Use All of Your Interests, Passions, and Hobbies to Create the Life and Career of Your Dreams
by Barbara Sher

Strength Based Leadership
by Tom Rath and Barry Conchie

Wishcraft: How to Get What You Really Want
by Barbara Sher and Annie Gottlieb

Zapp! The Lightning of Empowerment: How to Improve Productivity, Quality, and Employee Satisfaction
by William Byham and Jeff Cox

SAMPLE WORKSHEET: Mapping My Work History
DEPARTMENT

Finance

POSITION

Budget Analyst

SPECIALIZATION

Accounts Receivable, Payroll

EDUCATION

BA in Finance

SKILLS

Microsoft Excel, Microsoft Access, SAP, ERP

Ledgers, Quickbooks, Quicken

SUCCESSES & LESSONS

Improved organization of department was acknowledged (see attached letter)

Improved receivable rate by 20%

Learned the value of good client relationships with their key accounts people

Instituted more efficient payroll system and reduced time to complete

Made critical benefit information readily available to employees

SAMPLE WORKSHEET: Mapping My Work History
DEPARTMENT

Administration

POSITION

Secretary / Administrative Assistant

SPECIALIZATION

Meeting coordination, manage heavy phone calls for supervisor, client interface

EDUCATION

AA Degree

SKILLS

Microsoft Word, Microsoft Excel, Microsoft Outlook Meeting, One Meeting,
Netmeetings, GoToWebinar

SUCCESSES & LESSONS

Instituted better archiving system for phone messages

Coordinated annual out of state meeting of sales department; got rave reviews
(see attached letters)

Negotiated best rates for venue and lodging, saved company over $15,000

Feel very comfortable interacting with high-level clients (see attached Thank You
notes from several clients)

SAMPLE WORKSHEET: Mapping My Work History

DEPARTMENT

Safety

POSITION

Safety Engineer

SPECIALIZATION

OSHA Ordnance Procedures

EDUCATION

BA in Engineering

SKILLS

OP5 Explosive Arc Analysis

SUCCESSES & LESSONS

Increased safety compliance score by 20%

Eliminated all negative OSHA findings within two years on the job

Enhanced depth of safety training for all employee levels (see attached workbook that I created)

Sample Organizational Chart

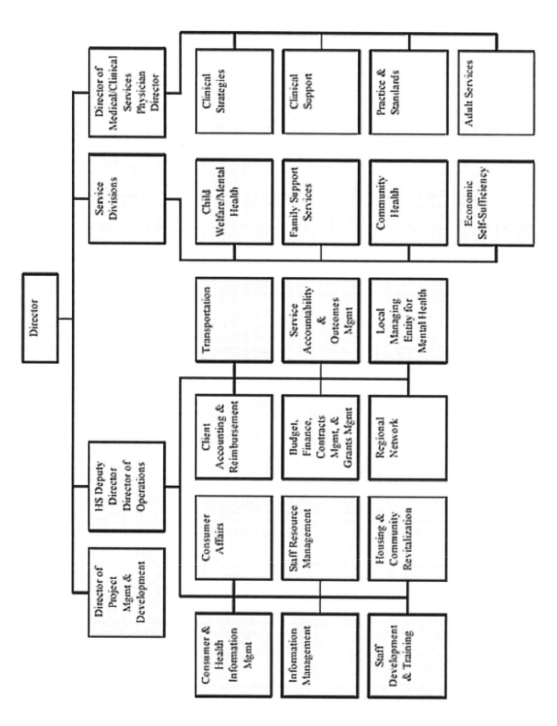

Acknowledgements

I would like to thank all my mentors and mentees over the years. We learned from each other.

Thanks to my editor, Oriana Green, who helped make the book relevant for a broader audience by contributing additional material.

Thanks most of all to those whose love sustained me, encouraged me and allowed me time away to document this process so that many others may benefit from it.

Carol Evanoff

You've probably heard about women who broke the glass ceiling—the barrier that kept women from advancing to the highest levels of corporate life. Carol Evanoff is one of those women, and now she's ready to share a lifetime of truly hard-earned wisdom to help others achieve their own dreams. There isn't a more male-centric work environment than a major defense contractor who supplies materials and services to the U.S. military, yet that's where Carol spent her entire 35-year career. She rose through the ranks from an hourly employee to supervisory then management positions. Along the way she earned her degree in management and attended numerous postgraduate institutes all across the country to study advanced leadership skills.

Throughout her career Carol often became the first woman to hold each new position she attained, and from the beginning, she made it her mission to help other women and minorities achieve the same level of success in their own careers. She's an award-winning innovator in executive leadership, change management, professional development and performance coaching. Her own success is measured by the professional success of over 1,000 colleagues and mentees she has guided. In her last position, Carol was the director of a large facility with vast responsibilities, supervised over 400 employees and managed an annual budget of $55 million. Yet she always found time to take a personal interest in creating programs to benefit her team as well as mentoring individual employees to reach their own dreams.

Recently retired from corporate life, she spends her time consulting, speaking to groups about career management, writing and enjoying life on Washington state's spectacular Olympic Peninsula. Through her efforts, major corporations, small businesses, leaders and individuals all create results-oriented and competitive differences in radically changing business environments.

Made in the USA
Middletown, DE
15 October 2015